To love is to listen...to listen is to love.

From a very early age Joanne has had an affinity with animals. a TV favourite after her appearances on shows such as *The Wright Stuff* & *The Sharon Osbourne Show*, her gift has helped thousands around the world to create a better relationship with their animals. As an Animal Communicator, Speaker & Animal Advocate, Joanne continues to help shine a light on the beautiful bonds that people and animals have with each other, showing that un-conditional love is real. Earlier this year Joanne was delighted to be invited to be a patron for 'Egypt Equine Aid' who do a fabulous job of helping horses and donkeys in Egypt. (egyptequineaid.org) Joanne currently lives in Warwickshire with her partner Dave and their two horses, four cats and two wonderful dogs.

Paws from the Past

JOANNE HULL

MINTFIELD BOOKS

Copyright © Joanne Hull 2017

First Published in Great Britain by Joanne Hull 2017
First published in paperback
by MINTFIELD BOOKS 2017

1

The right of Joanne Hull to be identified as the Author
of the Work has been asserted by her in accordance with the Copyright,
Designs and Patents Act 1988

All rights reserved. No part of this publication may be reproduced, stored in a retrieval system, or transmitted, in any form or by any means without the prior written permission of the publisher, nor be otherwise circulated in any form of binding or cover other than that in which it is published and without a similar condition being imposed on the subsequent purchaser.

All of the contributors in this book also gave full permission for their story to be told by Joanne Hull and cannot be reproduced, stored in a retrieval system, or transmitted, in any form or by any means without the prior written permission of the publisher

A CIP catalogue record of this book is available from the British Library

ISBN - 9781520236612

Although the advice and information in this book are believed to be accurate and true at the time of going to press, neither the author nor the publisher can accept any legal responsibility or liability for any errors or omissions that may be made nor for any inaccuracies nor any harm or injury that comes about from following instructions or advice in this book.

Mintfield Books
C/O 6 Mallow Croft
Bedworth
Warwickshire
CV12 0

Rest in peace furry angels
We will always love you

CONTENTS

Introduction

A life of love

My sweet Rosie

Pet's featured in this book;

Asterix, Frankie, Champers, Erni, Roman, Meri, Strider, Bobby, Gucci and Lucky, Kiwi, Topcat, Hal, Simba, Dino and Zara, Rosie, Gracie, Cassie and Sami, Poppy, Wild Geese, Bir-Bird, Jasper, Basil, Gypsie, Pippa, Stella, Thunder, Gina, Rizzo, Geronimo, Horatio, Zoe, TeddyBear Snarfles, Tiddles, Cassie, Fred, Blaze, Arnold, Tom, Oliver, Maisie, Teddy, Boudica, Dudley, Morrigan, Buster, Jack, Max, Banjo, Lucky, Ozzy, Bud, Morgan, Lulu, Abbey, Elsa, Spike, Moose.

Joanne's final words

Stages of grief

Acknowledgements

Joanne Hull

Authors note

Sitting here on my sofa, surrounded by my loved animals, my mind drifts into past times and I begin to remember those precious ones that I have sadly lost over the years, all of whom were special to me beyond words right now. For instance, my beautiful *'Rosie'* pictured above, was one of such animals that I had the pleasure or should I say the honour to share my life with. Rosie taught me what true un-conditional love really was.

Together we shared precious memories, tummy aching laughs, endless tears, nursed each other through illness and I shared secrets with her only she would ever hear, but most of all, we shared an amazing bond that I will never forget. When it was time for her to leave me, my world as I knew it fell apart. The gaping hole of grief that was felt within my heart was a heavy heartbreak to carry. Yet, slowly, in time, I was able to come to terms with my loss of the physical and remember all those precious times we spent together and I continue to celebrate her life to this day.

Rosie was one of the most beautiful dogs I have ever had the privilege to know and love. Our animals love is not one to disregard and I am quite sure those reading this will agree.

We may only ever experience one bond of un-conditional love from an animal during our lifetime.
Perhaps if we are lucky enough, we will connect with many, but one thing set in stone is that when grief hits us, it can hit us very, very hard, and to explain your feelings and sheer heartache to others is an almost impossible task. And so I set out on a quest to help and support those of you who may have lost animals in the past. Or maybe it is still yet to come. Always know that you are *not* alone.

This book is **not** my book, it never has been, it's yours; it is full of real life stories of love, loss and life after death. It features the animals in our lives and how each one made such a difference to us that we were truly affected by their passing. I hope I am able to show that the heartache does get better in time and that your grief does not define who you are but simply shows you that you have experienced a gift of un-conditional love so deep that it is to be championed and celebrated. I'd truly like to thank all the lovely contributors of this book, all of whom experienced grief and so gracefully agreed to share their experience for you today. I do hope their stories will help support you and bring some comfort in times of heartbreak. You will never forget your fur baby and why should you? But you will in time come to terms with your loss and something magical will begin to happen, the trauma of the loss will get less and less and the sheer beauty of the animal will shine in your heart like never before.
Peace will be found.
One last thing before we get started with this book and read some of the heartwarming real life stories that we have written for you, I would like to thank you so much for purchasing this book today, 'Thank you, Thank you, Thank you! Because, I'm not entirely sure you actually realize what you have just done? You, without maybe knowing it, have just helped support the animals that need us right now.

Because, every single penny of profit received through this book will go directly to those animals in need. Yes, I said it right! Every single penny! How amazing is that?

So, by purchasing this book today you are helping all types of animals to find loving partnerships just as you had with your animal. Isn't that wonderful? So enjoy and we all wish you love, peace and celebrated memories with your own animals.

A life of love

I could not put this book together without a little background on myself and why I have chosen to give all the proceeds from the sales to charity.

It all started many years ago when my love for animals grew beyond all expectations, you see, I had a unique gift and for some of you who have not yet heard about me yet, this may be a little bit of a surprise! Yes, I grew up with all the usual animals children do, but my relationship was different, really different, because I could really connect to them all on a deeper more intuitive level than most people. This meant that I could pick up feelings, thoughts and emotions and sometimes a video in my mind just like the ones you see on the TV screen, only now it was a playback of something the animal in question may had experienced in their lives.

All the above senses came from each animal I met. I was just a child who adored animals and it was totally normal for me to do all of the above, but as I grew up.

I soon realized my ability to connect with animals was different to most people, so this lead me to investigate and investigate I did.

There were many highs and lows, confusing and conflicting evidence, but, after lots of research and searching the world for similar experiences, I soon realized that what I was actually doing was called 'Animal Communication' and I certainly wasn't alone with my gift, there were in fact, many people around the world just like me!. So I suddenly realized my true life purpose was to help people and their animals create harmony within their relationships. I gave up a good career within Nestle to turn my skill into a full time job. My name soon became known nationally, then internationally and I was very quickly working with hundreds of clients around the globe and I loved it!

It wasn't long before I got noticed by a London literary agent and before I realized what was happening I had two books on the shelf at WH Smith, Waterstones and other book stores here in the UK. The first book called **'The Pet Psychic'** was my detailed story of how it all began for me and some amazing real life stories of my clients and their animals. I would also like to say that the publishers named this book, it really is a double edge sword so to speak, as the word *'psychic'* scares many people, yet all it means is an ability to use your intuition. It's certainly one of the most misinterpreted words out there today, I mean it's not like the ghost of old aunt Doris is going to walk through your door, it's nothing to be scared about at all, we all use our 'psychic' ability, probably daily, for instance, a mother will have that gut feeling or intuitive feeling that something is wrong with her child, even though the doctor may say he or she is fine, yet the mothers feeling will insist she pursues further investigation and nearly always, she is correct, and that the child turns out to be truly ill. This is called being 'Psychic, so calm down with the word a little, its fine ☺

My second book **'Puppy Tales'** was a celebration of dogs which also featured some real life stories from dog people and their connections
Both of which are still available to purchase on Amazon and other book outlets. Following my books came various TV appearances including slots as an animal expert on The Wright Stuff on Channel 5, appearing on The Sharon Osbourne Talk show, This Morning and a host of other mainstream shows on a regular basis. In fact, it was I that predicted via her cat, that Holly Willoughby the famous presenter and wonderful person was expecting her 2nd baby, I did this live on morning TV!

It was true of course and the press had a field day all around the world when Holly announced she was indeed pregnant just weeks after. I also wrote for two of the leading spiritual magazines, both 'Spirit & Destiny' and 'Soul & Spirit' as their monthly columnist and was included on many other leading magazine featured articles. After a couple of years, I took the decision to move away from the TV and magazines for a while to and concentrate on teaching others how to 'Communicate with Animals' which I have to be honest, has been absolutely amazing and I love nothing more than to see people follow their dreams and smash all the preconceptions of what is actually possible in this life. Many of my students from around the world have now made a full time career from 'Animal Communication' and I feel so proud to be a part of their own story.

Taking some time out, I needed to concentrate on my home life, which at that time was in utter turmoil for a while; in fact, I began to suffer really bad anxiety, panic attacks and swiftly fell into depression. I found life to be extremely difficult to navigate for a fair few years. Mental illness is a condition that can hit anyone at anytime, whether you are strong, naturally confident or quiet and reserved. So often we keep our feelings of losing control a secret.

And for me it all came out of the blue, like a bolt of lightning; it was like that huge lotto finger we see on TV, pointing right down on one of the strongest, most positive and energetic people I knew, who, in this case, turned out to be me!

My confidence and self esteem hit rock bottom and my ability to work and deal with clients was shot to pieces, my reputation was spiralling out of control, the trolls came out online and I almost crashed and burned. It was a struggle just to get up in the morning. I not only nearly lost my business, but I nearly lost myself, I could not see a future any more, I really couldn't.

But through it all, there was one consistent thing in my life that kept me going through the darkest of times, not once leaving my side, always making my cold heart from life's struggles warm up like somebody just turned up the thermostat in my body, it was those precious furry, often smelly, but super wonderful creatures, that I so lovingly shared my life with. Yes, my animals had started this whole journey of discovery for me and now they were still supporting me through my downfall, to be honest without them, I probably wouldn't be here writing this today, as life had packed its bags and left me for another it seemed, yet, having animals who depended upon me so much, made me get up, made me look after them and made me see why I had to keep going and not give up. I mean, how could I ever let them down when they had never let me down, my decision was nonnegotiable; I had to care for them. I had always been there for them and now I needed them more than I ever realized. They didn't let me down either, through their consistent un-conditional love and need for care; I slowly regained strength and gained the ability to overcome my mental health battle. To say it wasn't easy, is an understatement, but I feel truly blessed to have had the animals in my care at the time of my crisis. It is for this reason, I wanted to give something back.

I have other books to write, of course I do, in fact, I have many books swirling around in my mind at any given moment like a tornado waiting to choose its own new path, but I needed to write something now. Something which would help animals less fortunate, than mine. So, I put my brain to work and wondered if I could share some wonderful experiences that I have encountered with the animals during my lifetime.

Now there is lots I could share with you all regarding communicating with animals, but there is one particular subject that comes up over and over with my clients, something I myself have experienced numerous times over the years and this is the saddest area of keeping animals, we all know what I'm about to say I am sure, and that is, the dreaded death. But, thankfully, there are practical ways that you can recover from this grief, truly there are, so I hope throughout this little book, we can share this miracle of healing the heart with you. This book could have been written about almost anything that my work with animals covers, Missing pets, Mirroring, Behaviour, Care, Love etc yet the subject closest to so many hearts is the passing of our animals, so, it just had to be done. I decided to help both our two legged, four legged and even our 8 legged hairy friends by creating a book of love, hugs and stories of our precious animals ☺ and from the bottom of my heart I hope you love it as much as I have enjoyed putting it all together for you. So, settle down on the sofa, turn off all your TV's, radios, phones, Tablets (*unless you are reading this online of course lol*) and grab yourself a nice cuppa to settle down with and fill your soul with all the wonderful personal accounts of true animal connection through love, loss and life after passing to the other side. Be inspired by people's own stories, and know that whether you have already experienced the loss, or perhaps you are currently going through it, or know that one day it will grace your door, you are *NOT* alone.

For through these pages and from all our hearts (*I speak on behalf of everyone here of course*) we secretly hold your hand in friendship and send you the warmest of all heart hugs, support and most of all love.

One thing I must stress to you my friend, is that you are NEVER on your own with your grief that you suffer from.

My Sweet Rosie

As many of you have read my other books, you will already understand that I am right here with you sisters (*and brothers*) when it comes to losing them. Yes, the dreaded day comes to us all, but not a day goes past that I do not think of the animals that I have loved and have passed over in my life. I feel them or at least sense them, around me most of the time. If I am truly lucky, I will have one of those marvellous dreams where we are together again, always frolicking, having fun with plenty of hugs and kisses that melt your heart, but sadly the goodbyes inevitably must come, the ear-piercing noise from the alarm clock always jolts me out of my dream state bliss and back into reality. So often I give private readings for people who want to receive those all-important messages from their loved animals, it not only helps them understand that whilst our animals are passed over into to the world of spirit, they are very much still with us, sharing our lives, it also brings some well needed comfort, knowing that they are happy and safe. If I could wave a magic wand and show everyone that this world as we know it, through our human experience, is simply not what is out there in the big expanse that we call the universe.

I'd show them that our animals are here in the present, they can clearly hear us and even feel us. So just because they may be in a spirit body and not in that of a physical body, does not mean they have gone away. But until everyone understands this beautiful magic, I will continue to teach throughout the world, that the *'goodbye'* is only a word and that the *'hello'* from our beautiful furry, scaly, prickly, hairless, spiny, smelly, woolly friends is absolutely **FOREVER**. We never lose them, truly we don't and if we could only see through the tears of our heartache, we would be able to see the truth that the special time through the transition to the other side of life is a real-life miracle. Rosie, my beautiful Rosie, was one such example and as such I'd like to share her story with you if I may.

Now there is one thing we must be clear about here, it's that I LOVED her sooooooooo very much, I mean, the kind of love that connects you on the deepest level, the kind of love that people around you truly think you have lost your mind over this creature! You know, the type of love, where you would rather spend your days with them than anyone remotely human, the silly voices that only they would understand, their look of knowing that they heard exactly what you have just said even though you said it in your head. My nursing of her health back from the brink of death and praying to a god (*who sometimes made me ask the question if god is real then how on earth could he make my fur baby poorly in the first place!*). I'm mean if I did pray, he would surely keep her safe? Right? Well, I hoped so and prayed god was for real. You know that kind of love where your heart melts when you first lay eyes on their face, the moments you feel like you could kill someone if they were ever to try and hurt them.

Or the days when you take sides in an argument for the right of your animal to behave in a way that someone else doesn't agree with. Yes, we all know that love, now don't we?

The tears wiped away with a lick of their tongue or a nudge from their nose, the secrets you tell them and the moments of happiness you share whilst dancing around the room to their utter delight and wonder. The endless nights or days you snuggle in together for moments of true comfort, kindness and compassion. Yes my lovely friends reading this right now, you know what my love is... for my love is yours too!

The kind that is truly **un-conditional**. The kind that whilst humans try and perfect it over and over, it just simply is not possible and never will be, because something or someone will always trip them up – ALWAYS. You see, this was the type of love that I held for my Rosie. From the very first moment I laid eyes on her as a young puppy, I knew she was meant to be for me, she didn't look like a typical gangly Borzoi baby, or anything like her litter mates, in fact, Rosie looked like a little chubby short legged collie, honestly, she did. But knowing who her parents were, I knew she was just extremely special and thankfully under that collie disguise was a real Borzoi!

    I actually went to my friends to purchase Ruben my male Borzoi who was Rosie's litter brother, big, gangly, every bit the Borzoi puppy, and very much destined to be mine, he'd play, bounce and climb all over me. All the time the collie, or should I say Rosie, would climb and bite my clothing, tugging at my heart to take her too, whilst their litter mates who were quite obviously not impressed by my presence, all ran off to chase butterflies, bumble bees and other flying insects around the pretty English garden, whilst watched closely by their mum. There was no question in my mind, she *had* to come home with us, but, unfortunately, she had been booked to go to a home in America.

    I never gave up though and pestered and pestered my friends about Rosie being with Ruben and me, but they had to play fair to the other family and stick to what they had agreed, Rosie was to fly from the UK to America.

Later that month after I had collected little Ruben, I said goodbye to Rosie whispering in her ear that she should be with me, and I would have had her in my care in a split second if I could.

I was at a dog show with my other older and most handsome Borzoi Mozart when I got a tap on my shoulder. It was my friend, Rosie and Ruben's breeder, 'Joanne' she said 'You know the family who were taking Rosie? well the deal fell through, so would you like her?' Like her???? OMG! I think at that moment I nearly fell off the show ring chair! And without any hesitation I said a big fat whoop whoop YES! I was beside myself in happiness.

So, that was how Rosie came to me, oh, I missed out a slight bit of information here, which I guess is one very important one, you see, all along I had told Rosie she should be with me, all along I wished that she was with me and all along I thought she should be with me, yet all the odds were stacked against us. Why?

Well firstly, she was booked for America, secondly, I had room for one puppy, not two, thirdly my then partner Fraser would have had a massive meltdown if I had purchased two very expensive puppies at once and fourthly, well OK, I couldn't afford two, I mean seriously, I had saved up every last penny I had to purchase Ruben. Yet I knew at that moment it was a BIG FAT **YES**! She would finally be mine ♥

Sometimes, life has a way of throwing you the perfect curve ball, a ball of opportunity and this moment was just one of those times. I had to think quickly, I mean where the hell was I going to get over six-hundred pounds at a drop of a hat and I knew Fraser would say no.

The universe gave me a huge lifeline, you see this glorious bundle of fun was meant for me, I knew it, she knew it, the universe knew it and her breeders knew it.

At the time, I remembered a conversation with my friends about needing more food for their dogs and at the time I also happened to work for one of the leading pet food companies who manufactured a super premium food called Pro plan, something many of you may have heard of.

Each month, we were given lots of odd bags that were close to sell by date or that we had been given back by shop keepers because of damaged packaging etc, now normally you were told 'just use it or disperse of it, (in other words bin it!) because it would cost the company too much to post back, it was just not cost effective I guess. I tried many times to give it away to both friends and rescue centres, but storage always came up as the number one issue, so I used to bring the large sacks home and keep them in my garage in case anyone I knew wanted any.

But today was my chance to negotiate, you see my friends always purchased theirs from their local representative in huge quantities (As they had a lot of dogs) which cost them a small fortune to feed.
So, seeing an obvious opportunity I piped up 'What about if I give you food to the equivalent of the cost of Rosie, that way you have food for the dogs and I can have the pup, it's a win, win situation and of course you can have more food as I have lots available if you can store it.?' I remember holding my breath for a few seconds as my idea sunk in...'It's a deal' she said and that was that! Rosie was all mine! Rosie licked my nose and cuddled into me all the way home and greeted her little brother with and equally big kiss and a chase around the garden like she was finally home.

We shared so many happy memories together over nine years or so, she was not only one of the most wonderful dogs I have ever met, she was also a beautiful and gentle soul with a wicked sense of humour! In fact, I miss her so much, remembering her gentleness, the softness of her coat and her sheer beauty which pulls at all my heart strings constantly.

Rosie gave me companionship, a partner if you will and especially that one thing us humans crave, 'un-conditional love', she couldn't care less if my breath was stinking or my clothes were muddy from mucking out the horses, or that I was hung over from the night before! All she wanted from me was ... ME!

She showed me what true love was and how no matter what goes on in our lives whether we are broke, hungry or riding high on the tide of success, she was 100% <u>consistent</u> in her love. There were no bargaining chips, for example 'I will love you more if you lose a little weight' or 'When you get that job, then you will have more to give' etc, No, she just loved me for just being me.

We spent so many fond times travelling up and down the country participating in championship shows, which I may add she won most of! Yes, not only was she an amazing soul but that little collie looking dog grew up to be one of the UK's finest Borzoi's in the breed. She won so much over the years that I've actually lost count, but put it this way, she was a multi champion and a regular winner at Crufts the World's biggest dog show. Rosie loved travelling and showing which I guess is a huge bonus for me, I would never have pursued it if she hadn't wanted to be there, not like little Ruben who became a couch potato and was quite happy barking us *goodbye* at the weekends so he could have the most comfortable dog bed to himself without Rosie claiming it first, after all she was the boss ☺

My time with this precious girl meant everything to me, even those times when she used to wait till our eyes were closed at bedtime, so she could step quietly towards the hotel table and eat our following days sandwiches in silence or when she pulled the door frame of a hotel room in literally one minute because I took a phone call in the corridor and she couldn't be with me!

Or the time she decided to poke her head through our fence in a flash of rage at the tormenting postman and not so gently took hold his hand in her jaws! (*Did I say she was gentle?*)

Yes, I'd give anything to have her back in her physical body with me again. But, I'm afraid like so many others that will never happen. You see on a day I least expected it, my beautiful Rosie was involved in what I can only call a tragic *but* avoidable accident at home. She had been quite poorly with arthritis for some time, having gained weight after an operation when she was younger, and so as she grew old for a Borzoi (average age nine to twelve years) the weight just wouldn't shift, this lead her to become extremely immobile, she found it difficult to get up after laying down, walking was difficult and her back legs and lower back were becoming more and more weak. Obviously, I helped every day to make sure she was as comfortable as possible and her wagging tail and soft kisses always kept my faith in the fact when the time came, she'd let me know.

However, what happened that day will stay with me forever, we had been doing some decorating and the two dogs were laying in their beds, opposite them rested a pair of metal ladders, just temporarily, leaning against the wall, waiting to be placed on the next part for decorating, something we have always done. I will regret for the rest of my days the forthcoming event, it all happened in such a flash that even recalling the moment for you today is a little blurry. In fact, I don't think I have ever told anyone the full story outside my close family and friends, so trust me when I say it's so difficult to share, but with the guilt I felt and the understanding now, I hope it helps others to overcome their own feelings of 'what if's?'.

We had just walked into another room to fetch something, when we heard our cats have a moment of disagreement with each other, which is nothing unusual from time to time.

Then immediately after a clang of metal and an almighty crash, followed by the deep sound of extreme pain that I will never forget. Racing immediately back into the room to my horror. I saw Rosie trapped under the ladders, the same ladders that a moment ago was safely leaning against the wall opposite, until one of the cats had taken a flying leap up onto the top step in order to escape the cat fight, in doing so, she had pushed the ladders away from the wall and toppled the metal treads onto my girl, who at the time could not manage to move quick enough out of the way due to her mobility issues. As she had tried to move out of the way, the ladders came crashing down and landed on her spine and in an instant, paralysed her completely.

I write this through tears with 'what if the ladders were somewhere else?' 'Why did we put them there?' 'It's my fault,' etc. As I lifted the ladders away and sobbed over her, she wagged her tail whilst looking at me through painful eyes, she had no more use of her legs. Rosie kissed and licked my tear stained face as I tried to help her, but I could see she was damaged beyond help.

Before I knew what was happening the vet was checking her over, doing tests and talking to me with dread in her voice, to be quite honest most of the words were just white noise to my ears as I buried my face into Rosie's soft fur, whispering that I loved her more than life itself.

The vets settled her into a room on a soft bed, and we were to come back first thing to check on how she was doing after they tried everything to help her stand up. But sadly, she never did.

The next morning I knew what was to come, she gave me the biggest kiss and helped me understand that her time on this earth as a physical dog had finished and so without a hesitation through my tears I asked the vet to allow her to go.

I didn't want her to suffer any more, she couldn't stand up, she was a large dog and was losing her dignity due to her not being able to go to the toilet and that there had been no movement at all in her legs, she had in fact been paralysed and the spine too badly injured for any recovery. I could not see her suffer any more, she was ready and so was I. Rosie had been my best friend and now I had to do the right thing for her. This was not about me anymore. I kissed her gently for the last time as the needle entered the vein in her leg, as I sat back a huge feeling of love came over me, her eyes closed and the vet checked her heart and through the tears I could see a shadow of her body slowly rise up as if moving towards the ceiling, I wiped my eyes and it had gone, so too had my tears, I knew at that moment she was absolutely free and I shouted as if to give her one last message 'I love you Rosie, I'm so sorry' and felt the immediate love right back. I looked down and saw her lifeless body, a shell, of who she was. The beauty of course was still very much there, the long velvet nose, the soft wavy red and white coat and one of her paw pads gently pressed up against me. I wrapped her in her quilt and took her body home with us. I knew I had seen her leave, I knew the shadow of her leaving was to let me know she was ok and I knew I could never love a dog so much.

    Rosie was one of those animals that come into your life and change you forever, she was my world and yes, I have loved so many and probably will love so many more, but my little collie like puppy that lived to a grand old age for a Borzoi was one in a million.

The circumstances of her death still haunt me and the guilt and the 'what ifs' never truly go away, but it does get easier as time moves on. I wonder sometimes, was it all for a reason? Did those ladders enable her to go when she needed to because her other conditions were restricting her quality of life so much?

And knowing what I know about animals and their passing, I'd like to say yes, it was all meant to happen that way. But does it feel any better?
No, why?
Because I miss her, so very much and always will. She was the most beautiful Borzoi I have ever had the pleasure to share my life with.

And I loved her. ♥

Asterix

By

Brimble Wharton

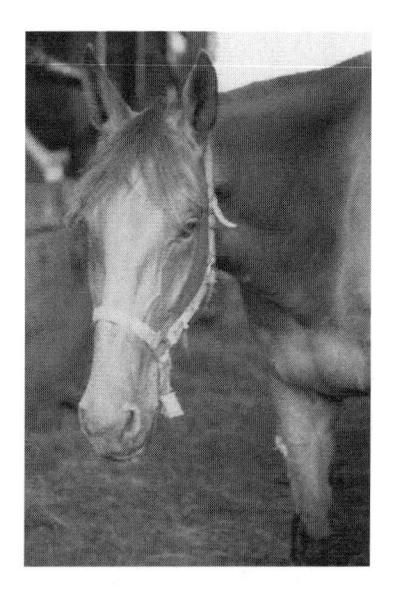

I met Asterix when I was living in south west France with my partner back in 1992. I was then twenty-two, and Asterix was just three years old. I was taken to the yard where he was stabled, by a local who was showing me around the area. The place was dismal and depressing. A yard for failed or broken racehorses, the trainer buying them cheap as they couldn't run, yet held valuable qualification papers.

He attempted to patch them together and begin working them as soon as possible. I was shown Asterix. I immediately felt extreme sadness for him.

He was so tall, and beautiful with the most sensitive face and eyes, yet his head hung low as he stood hunched up at the back of the tiny filthy stable, every rib and vertebra protruded. I had never seen such a thin horse, except in RSPCA type appeals.

He didn't move. Patches of sweat were forming on his ultra fine coat, and he looked anxious but also with a look of bewilderment and great sadness in his eyes. As I peered over the battered old door, which had a rusty strand of electrified barbed wire across it, I could see he was standing in deep filth. The stable was so small he could barely turn around, and he was too afraid and shut down to even move. A half empty water bucket in the corner was black from dung which had fallen in, by the looks of it, some time ago. It was a boiling hot day, and the atmosphere was hot, oppressive, filthy and truly hellish. There were rows of small rickety stables with broken horses all hiding like tortured prisoners within them.

The trainer explained in his macho way, how Asterix had qualified and run some big races, but that his jaw had been smashed and broken, and he had problems with his back. As he couldn't run, he was sold very cheaply from the professional yard. The new trainer ignored veterinary advice about resting him long term. Instead he was made to immediately begin training again.

This had been going on for a few weeks, but by now Asterix had virtually stopped eating. He was lame, and was obviously in considerable pain.

There was talk of him being taken away to a big market in Toulouse, where he would either fetch the attention of another trainer interested in his papers alone, or else one of the multitude of butchers.

Whilst the others chatted and talked, I returned to Asterix's stable door. I felt such a profound sadness as I gazed over at him, my hands in my pockets and by now my head also hanging low. I knew he had been through hell already, and was still only a baby, and I feared greatly for his future. He slowly uncomfortably shifted his weight from one front foot to the other, and our eyes met as he took a slow sideways glance towards me, and I shall never forget that moment. I went home and couldn't stop thinking about him. I knew he was in such pain both emotionally and physically and so much at the mercy of people who could neither recognise this, nor even cared to. To them he just represented a blank cheque. Within a week, I had spoken to everyone. The timing was right, and he was soon delivered to the little vineyard where we lived with my other horses.

From that day onwards and for the next twenty-three years, Asterix would be with me wherever I lived, moving with me to many different places, including across the sea to England. He was always going to be vulnerable, and I made him know that I would never ever send him away or sell him. I would always love and protect him. I rested him for nearly two years, allowing him to grow and heal. We then went for long walks, me on foot by his side, sharing the beauty of nature and the countryside, meeting wild boar in forests, along little lanes and through villages.

Whenever he was nervous I would talk to him, reassuring him that together we could face anything.

Eventually I began riding him, and later together we learnt dressage, and did some wonderful pleasure endurance rides. I always felt like a lottery winner riding him in public. He was so stunning and beautiful. People would often comment on his grace and presence. Aside from being my riding horse, he was also a profoundly special friend. He witnessed all the major key events in my adult life, welcoming each of my four babies as they arrived home for the first time, and being my soul mate he knew always what was happening in my life. He knew how much I needed his loving when my Mum died. He would literally wrap his neck around my body and hold me there. He let me sob into his warm soft neck and offered me a kind of peace that I could find nowhere else on earth.

When my son was ill (for several years), he was my rock. He always knew how I was feeling, and could offer me just the right amounts of gentleness, humour and sensitivity, depending on how badly things were going. I always knew how deep my love for him was, but until he was gone, I never knew just how much I relied on him. He was like a best friend, soul mate, uncle, brother and father all rolled into one. The day that I lost him was the very worst day of my life. I had been away in London where my son was in hospital. My husband had been doing all the usual feeding and watering and all had reportedly been well the day before.

I returned home for a whistle-stop 24-hour midweek visit, to give the horses and my other children some extra TLC. As I went to bring the horses in from their field, everyone apart from Asterix was by the gate. This instantly rang alarm bells, because he led the herd always, and was always the first to arrive. I could see him standing at the bottom of the field, seemingly unable to move.

My heart in my mouth, I quickly took the others in, and ran back down the hill to see what could be the matter. By now he was trying very hard to walk towards me. He looked gravely unwell. He could barely put one foot in front of the other, he was sweating, but perhaps most alarming of all was that his eyelids seemed to droop over his eyes in the most unnatural way. I almost couldn't recognise him. I feared he had maybe suffered a stroke. Slowly I managed to guide him to his stable in the barn. He went to take a drink from his water bucket, but to my horror, I could see he wasn't able to swallow. He went to his manger to try and eat the treats waiting, but again couldn't even chew or swallow. He lay down to roll on his bed, clearly having colic, and clearly in pain. I called the vet who came quickly. I knew he needed urgent medical attention, but never did I believe I would now lose him forever.

The vet was swift, thorough, professional and very sensitive, for which I am eternally grateful. He examined Asterix, and explained how his stomach was paralysed. His eyelids too were paralysed. His pulse was 90. He was very seriously ill and in pain, with sudden onset acute grass sickness (akin to botulism poisoning from the soil...though it is little understood) The vet explained there was no cure and that he would die a slow death within 24-hours, and that the only kind thing we could do for him was put him to sleep as soon as possible.

He gave him morphine and sedated him, so at least he could spend his final precious minute's pain free and in a state of calm. I was in deep shock. It had all happened so quickly and suddenly, and nothing could have prepared me.

It's hard to express in words the emotions I felt during that hour. The vet sympathetically went away to his car and left me alone with Asterix for ten minutes so I could say goodbye to him in private. I didn't know where to begin! My whole face felt numb and I couldn't speak. All I was able to do was wrap my arms around his neck, for this one final time. I wanted so much to reassure him, to tell him that I loved him and always would do, and to thank him with all my heart for all our precious years together. I was too grief stricken to speak. Tears poured down my contorted face.

The best I could do was to make as little sound as possible, as I hugged and hugged and hugged him. Strangely there was an unusual silence in the barn. The radio had stopped working. The other horses didn't move in their stables, and even the birds seemed to stop singing. The vet reappeared, and I knew it was time. Very slowly I led Asterix out of the barn for the final time. As he passed his little wife Ginger, our Welsh mountain pony (who he had adored for twelve years, and never let out of his sight) she called out to him. I was so blinded by tears I literally couldn't see where I was going. I led him out to his favourite patch of grass behind the barn. The vet slowly and carefully described what he was going to do and what would happen. I was glad Asterix had been heavily sedated, as I was so scared he would understand what was about to happen to him.

The vet administered the drug, and like a magnificent tree Asterix slowly fell to the ground. I was assured he would be totally unconscious before he even reached the ground. Watching his body going down was like slow motion for me, and one of the most profoundly heartbreaking moments of my life.

There is something so powerful about watching a big horse go down in its final moments (not sleepy and easy like perhaps a cat already lying comfortably) and when it is your best friend wrapped in this mighty body, it's even more upsetting. Moments later I heard him take his last breath. It was the little purring sound he would make through his big velvet nostrils sometimes and the reason his nickname had always been pussy cat.

Our twenty-three years together on this earth had come to an end. My heart felt like it had been broken into a million pieces.

The vet quietly left, and I lay by Asterix's side for several hours until the sun began to set, stroking his fetlock and talking to him through a never-ending river of tears. The next day we buried him and held a full family funeral. His little wife Ginger has also since died and she is now buried next to him.

There isn't a day that goes by that I don't talk to the pair of them. I look for little signs, and sometimes I feel music has been sent with messages within. There are also two robins who visit regularly. One sits on the wall to Asterix's stable every single morning, and the other sits up high above Gingers stable and sings so loudly. Ginger was the most vocal little pony I have ever known. I like to think and do believe these robins are connected to their spirits. For many weeks after I lost Asterix, I found it hard to function at all. I wore dark glasses everywhere I went, and going into the barn was desperately painful, but I had to do it, because the other horses were also grieving and they needed a lot more extra love and care than usual.

It's been over two years since I lost Asterix now.

I still struggle and still shed tears. Things like his rugs and his stable can set me off, but I say goodnight to him every single night when I tuck the others in. Slowly I've found that life goes on, and though I will always and forever miss him, life is becoming more bearable, with the inevitable acceptance and healing that time brings. I did find homeopathic Ignatia remedy extremely helpful, through my darkest hours. I also had some of his hair put into a beautiful pendant which I also had engraved. I wear this when I need to feel close to him. I also planted two fruit trees and lots of wild flowers over his grave.

I learnt so much about how other horses cope with grieving also, and just how much support they can need. My little veteran Shetland has always been the wise old lady of the family, but she went through some very dark days, definitely shedding tears in her heart, and finding it hard to carry on. My other big old French racehorse was also traumatised. Asterix had been his first and only real friend, after years of being institutionalised in racing. He behaved in a very physical way, pacing around his stable, also, for many days; desperately wanting to sniff the ground where Asterix had lay down. He was much quieter than usual, and was definitely struggling to come to terms with his own loss. If there was one thing I would want to tell Asterix, I'm sure that like most others, it would be that I love him.

I have always loved him and I always will do. I treasure his memory and will never forget him, not ever. I would want to thank him for his deeply precious kind ways, his wisdom, courage, faith, humour and for all the magical and profound things he taught me.

I hope he's still around me, and I hope he isn't sad about things, and most of all I hope he feels surrounded by love every second of every day and night....and that I'm living in his light.

I will love you forever Asterix ♥

FRANKIE

By

Tracey Cooke

It's funny how you look back at certain times, certain characters and certain events of your life that reached out and touched you and made you the person you are today. Even moments that at the very time they were happening seemed unfair or unjust as we reflect upon them, we realize it was all synchronized, all meant to be exactly the way it happened, the way it was supposed to play out and become woven into your life your memories your soul.

This story is of such an event that gave me the gift to realize that sometimes just simply loving someone is enough. It all began one unbearably hot Friday afternoon in Burbank. I was leaving work and heading home in my beat up old Volkswagen called Archie. Poor Archie had seen better days; I didn't need a key to start him, he had a switch rigged up to his fuel pump relay, one flip and Archie god willing, on a good day, would start.

He was a bit temperamental mind you. Oh dear, well enough of Archie and his wicked ways, I am straying. I was only trying to make a point that it was bloody hot and to stop Archie overheating I had to put the heater on full blast, cars don't tell me they don't have a mind of their own.

Well, less than 5 minutes into my journey home as my mind was wondering which way to go, (we had recently moved to the house from hell.

The agency that showed the property took us in the scenic route, leaving us oblivious that we were actually in the middle of gang territory, we soon became aware once we had signed the lease and made our own way home, the rather un-scenic way that was right around the corner from our new home!) A voice alerted me *"You are a hazard on the road!"* the policeman shouted from a load speaker opposite me, rousing me from my thoughts *"you! …. you are a hazard … that car is a hazard"* he shouted again at me! Oh god, he was shouting at me and everyone was looking and my stomach began churning. *"fix your indicators!"* boomed the voice and I nodded red from the shame as I didn't have insurance and was grateful to escape without him stopping me.

I was actually relieved to be almost home, I had decided to take the un-scenic route past the apartments with the old sofas in the streets and past the broken-down cars that made Archie look like a Rolls Royce. 'I'm almost home, thank heavens' I thought. Then out of the corner of my eye to my horror, I see a tiny little body walking slowly on the sidewalk, I slowed down the car to see him clearly and saw his head down, sad, lonely and I felt his sadness. I watched him slowly walking, tired, just so tired, I knew he was thinking 'WHY, why can't anyone love me? I watched that frail thin little cat and hoped halfway that he would turn into a driveway but he didn't. I watched as an old man 'shoo shooed' him away from his gate just for simply walking by. I pulled up beside him and got out I stroked his coat gently, god he was frail and thin, in a real bad way. All the while he never moved from my touch. He wanted to be held even if it was just for that moment. I guess I did too. Well what could I do? I had no option, you see I couldn't leave him, so I placed him in the car

(Which felt like a million degrees by now) and me and the cat I named 'Frankie', which by the way turned out to be a bad choice of name, became friends.

Frankie use to creep everyone out, which I found quite amusing, all because he had just a few teeth left, which were brown and gnarled. What fur he had left, had seen better days too! Even the dogs, who were both huge, were petrified of him and didn't dare touch their food until he had grazed upon the plate first and took what he could suck up or attempt to chew on. He didn't like anyone but me and growled like a dog if anyone went near him, we were an odd pair, everyone made fun of him and called him Frankenstein (told you bad choice of name … hindsight huh!)

The months passed and we moved from our gang land abode after a flood and the worst infestation of Chinese cockroaches the exterminator had ever seen. For those of you who have never seen these giant cockroaches, they are BIG and I mean BIG, they are also perfectly happy to join you in the shower, making surprise visits up the plug hole whilst inviting the whole family along for a dip with them. Our swimming pool also became theirs and theirs alone, as they basked in it in their hundreds, like some sort of giant cockroach family holiday! So, with a huge sigh of relief, we moved back to Burbank.

One day, a few months after we moved Frankie, he didn't show up for breakfast and I worried about him as I drove to work. At about 11am I had an overwhelming urge to go home, I can't really explain it to be honest; it was just a real urge, so I took my lunch early and headed back. My stomach churned as I pulled up outside to see the animal control van already there, the man was carrying a wrapped-up bundle to the van! My heart sank, I just knew it was Frankie!

He was dead!

I took him swiftly from the man and held him to me, my eyes filled with tears, he had just started growing back his fur a beautiful burgundy brown colour and now my precious boy was gone forever. I buried him that day and I felt so very lost without him.

Everyone else that had met Frankie breathed a sigh of relief and had no qualms of showing it either, they no longer had to face him, but to me, he was perfect. This poem is what I wrote for my Frankie, as I never managed to capture any photographs of him. I will never forget the days we had together,

I love you Frankie ♥.

IN MEMORY OF FRANKIE BY TRACEY COOKE

All they saw was a tattered old rag
A can kicked and smashed in the road
A chair by a dumpster, broken and unwanted
Looking with eyes empty and lost
All they see is what's left
Not what was or could ever be
Your beautiful eyes that shone like a star
Bright with devotion with love always wanted
With a need to feel love, is that so different than you, than me?
He was proud, a fighter, tough mangled, hard as nails
Torn ears, barely hanging like a Childs favourite teddy bear
Bones clinging to his skin tightly, holding on for dear life
I wanted to wrap that pained little body in a red flag of courage
For inside that broken body that shell he had to live in
Inside that smashed can was a rainbow
So bright and beautiful, if only they could see
But when you are blind to someone else's need you don't see that rainbow
All you chase is the gold at the end
Where does it lay? Well, I found it without looking
I picked up that tattered rag that broken chair
That smashed can you all saw
And I found more beauty
More love more peace than you
All of you who turn a blind eye will ever know.

Champers

By

Brenda Oakley-Carter

Champers - 23/4/1982 - 19/5/2003

I first met Champers as a little kitten. He was a very pale ginger (he was almost champagne colour, hence his name) and seemed laid back and not busy like the other kittens around him. I connected and fell for him straight away and that was the beginning of a friendship that was to last for twenty-one wonderful years!

Champers seemed an 'old soul' even when he was young. He had a 'knowing' about him, a determination and independence that was his very essence. He wasn't a lap cat but very loving in his own way. Champers was always there for me.

As he got older his kidneys started to fail but he soldiered on determinedly. In 2002 when he was twenty, he was diagnosed with a malignant melanoma on his nose.

I was told there was nothing that could be done as he was too old and the melanoma was too far advanced, however, Champers was not ready to give up. As the wound on his nose got progressively worse I took him to the vet who told me Champers life expectancy was very short, in fact he thought he might have to put him down the following week as he couldn't do anything else for him. After a tearful journey, as I was wondering what else I could do for him, he jumped up and sat on my lap, which was unlike him, as he wasn't really a lap cat. It slowly dawned on me that he was there because I needed to give him Reiki. He stayed with me for two hours. This was an exceptional amount of time as a cat will usually take between twenty and forty minutes Reiki.

The same thing happened the following day, and by the end of the weekend the wound was clean, had healed over, and the smell of decay that was always there had gone. Naturally there were relapses in the months that followed, as he was very old, but with a combination of surgery to clean and stitch the wound, homeopathy and regular Reiki, Champers was still able to enjoy life. Champers had been getting weaker, wobblier and was struggling to get to the kitchen to eat. He was getting more and more snuffly as the 'hole' on his face got bigger and he started being sick after he ate.

I knew it was time was when he pooed on the kitchen floor and didn't realise. He also lost his balance and almost fell out of the litter tray...his dignity was going and the struggle was too much although he kept on trying to the very end. It was so very difficult to ring the vet and I sat at home and waited with Champers for the vet to come.

We sat together quietly, Champers dozing happily on his favourite chair and me just stroking him, giving him Reiki and telling him it was all ok, thanking him for being with me and how I'd always love him and that I'd be fine.

He lived on for nearly a year after the vet had given up on him. He finally passed away at the age of twenty=one.
He was with me longer than anybody in my life. I felt very alone suddenly and was so very, very upset. My dear old boy who showed me to never give up and keep trying wasn't there but I'd just met the wonderful man who was going to be my husband and it was almost like Champers knew he could safely leave me at last.

I have a fond memory of him; it was a day that I was moving house and Champers was nowhere to be found. Time was getting on and the van was packed up and ready and I'd been calling and calling him for hours...but nothing, not a sign of him. I'd just arranged with my neighbour who knew him well to get him into her house when he came back and ring me immediately when he came strolling around the corner in his ploddy old way, without a care in the world! I was SO overjoyed to see him and he was so nonplussed about it all.

One piece of advice about pet loss... The bond can never be broken as the love goes on. Grieve for as long as you need. Don't let people tell you it's only an animal, because those that do just do not understand. Thank you Champers for our time together.

I love you ♥

Erni

By

Janette Rayton

Erni, my dog had been fighting kidney failure for a year and a half, we spent 4 days a week in the vets and bless him, he got so accepting of the tablets and injections but he hated going in the vets he would grumble and be known as their favourite grump!.

Anyway, sadly he developed anaemia then pancreatic disease, even through with all this, he still battled on and the vets said he wouldn't last much longer, so advised us in their opinion that the time had come to be put to sleep. The news was devastating, but I just couldn't do it, so I took him home and he actually perked up a little, I didn't want to lose him, he was everything to me. I never left his side for two weeks solid, but I did do the right thing and that was to ask him to let me know when it was his time to go, I knew that he could do this for me as our bond and connection was so strong.

He was so cuddly and loving that evening, he could hardly walk, but he wanted to take me somewhere, it was strange, he had a type of determination that I had not seen before.

So, I popped his collar and lead on and let his lead go longer as he pottered over to the car, it was 2am in morning and he looked at me to get us to go, I knew he meant, it was the vets, it was time and we both knew it. The signal was obvious, so through tears, I took him to the vets and he didn't even grumble or fuss, which was certainly not like him, this just confirmed what I felt in my heart was true.

When we got to the place, he was great, now this was highly unusual, because he would never normally go in willingly, but this time, he was so different, he knew.

It was time. So, I said my goodbyes as I wrapped him in his blanket. There was no doubt in my mind I was doing the right thing, he had made it quite clear and I had to respect his wishes. I requested his ashes to be in a beautiful casket with the words engraved on it saying;

ERNI my angel
YOU LIVE ON IN THE HEARTS YOU LEAVE BEHIND.

That morning, I went to work and looked up in the sky and there to my surprise was a cloud exactly in the shape of my Erni when he was young, it also remained long enough for me to take a picture and then it was gone. Over the next few months and every Wednesday since the 30th June when Erni passed over, I receive a heart or three hearts with the number 3 on, some signs are petals in the shapes of hearts or stones on the beach. We went to a Chinese restaurant and our table was the only one with hearts above as decoration and a heart candle holder all the others were birds I found in the cupboard a heart trinket with a Westie on it. Also, there was a pack of playing cards with three hearts and a heart gift bag and a little dog wearing heart glasses!

On a walk recently, there was a leaf pinned on a telegraph pole, I noticed it was in the shape of a heart and the road sign had a heart sticker too, these all started to appear like signs from Erni. Even the chair I sat in at the bingo hall had a carved heart on it and the hotel I stayed at had a shower head with engraved hearts in it and that night the moon above my head was in a perfect heart shape.

All these signs keep happening all the time, they come out of nowhere. It could just be coincidence, but I swear it's him. I know he has taken his words on his casket;

'You live on in the hearts you leave behind'

We love you Erni ♥

Roman

By

Amanda Long

I had Roman from 9 weeks old; he was a very special loyal loving boy, a beautiful German Shepherd dog. He knew me as well as I knew him. He was my rock through many changes in my life.

On the morning he passed, I'd booked the day off work because he was so poorly. He didn't sleep the night before and it was heartbreaking seeing him so restless, he stayed in the bedroom with me. I got up early the next morning to be with him.

He was so very tired, so I took the water bowl to him for him to have a drink, after he drank the water he wanted to go out, so I went with him slowly into the garden. We stood for a while as he looked around his garden, I asked him if he wanted to sit down and he did, then he lay down gently, I was behind him on my knees talking to him all the time. He then seemed to become a little confused as to where he was, looked at me, leaned into me for a hug and then gave a deep breath and passed away. As heartbreaking as it was at that moment, for I had lost my most beautiful boy, I was relieved for him because of the restless night before that he'd had. Thankfully I'd decided to have him home for the weekend after he'd been to the specialist for tests. This was a blessing, so he passed away at home with me by his side. A month or so later my mother in law went to a spiritual evening at a local centre. The lady 'Kath Logan' walked up to my mother in law and said "I have the biggest most beautiful German shepherd here called Roman!" My Mother in law was astounded and said that he's my daughters? Kath replied "I know, he just wants her to know that he's ok."

I have also seen and heard him around the house many times which brings me great comfort. We often think they have gone forever, when in fact Roman has proved there is life after death many times over to me, this is something wonderful to hold on to.

They do not leave us, they simply move into a different form. I am lucky to have seen and heard from my boy, something I hold very dear to my heart as a blessing from above.

I love you Roman.♥

Meri

By

Gemma Wilson

In Memory, of 'Meri' also known as 'America' 26th April 1992 to 24th April 2011.

We lost our gorgeous Meri our beautiful, loyal Arabian mare four years ago to extensive changing cancerous melanomas, she was in our lives for four and a half years.

Soon after buying her, we discovered she had a few melanomas which replicated over time through metastasis, they soon started to occur and she was soon riddled with huge ones in compromising places. We made her as comfortable and happy as we could in the short last few years of her life, we purchased her last colt foal too and she lived with him right until her passing. I believe this mare was meant to be ours despite her condition; she helped us as much as we tried to help her through the bad times in ours and her life. Just being in the radius of this beautiful mare always lifted our spirits and gave us hope when we felt there was none.

I would honestly recommend a pet bereavement service to anyone who has lost a beloved pet. It's no different from losing a family member with the whirlwind of emotions that continue on for some time afterwards. I accept that I was right to end my mares suffering at the time. I would never have passed her on to an unknown fate or anyone else.

I hope that when I pass she will meet me in that place where we pass on, free of what was plaguing us here.

I love you 'Meri' ♥

Strider

By

Sally Higgins

I could go on forever how special dear Strider was but will try and sum him up for you.

We got him as a three-month-old puppy when we were at a local horse show and someone I sort of knew was there with a lovely Lurcher puppy (Strider's brother) of course. I loved him, what's not to love about these sweet natured hounds. Our eldest cat Satchmo a very chilled black moggie had sadly recently died and as I was no longer working full time and had always wanted a dog, it just felt like the right time. My husband was not keen, but was soon won over when this little tiger striped puppy was plonked on his lap. Strider (woof was pet name) soon became one of the family, he used to Gallop upstairs with my boys and their friends and sit between them all when they played on the Playstation. He was just one of the boys! He took it in turns which of the boy's beds he would sleep on and even used to climb onto a desk chair and then climb up onto my youngest son Troy's bed which was up higher.

Strider adored other dogs and was very bouncy and playful. After having him a few years, along came Rox another Lurcher his adopted sister, they were great pals and he was very tolerant of Rox being a bouncy puppy.

For about six months leading up to his death, we were going backwards and forwards to the vet with him as he had a lump on his side which was misdiagnosed cancer. He had a wonky walk as a couple of years before he had a back injury which left him with nerve damage which complicated matters, but he still did everything he did before and kept up charging around with Rox.

Eventually when he had just turned nine, I begged the vets to investigate further I really felt he was suffering. The last time I took him to the vets expecting to pick him up later, I got the dreaded phone call. I had to make the horrid decision to let him go, feeling that it would be far two distressing for all of us to bring him round to say goodbye. But on a lighter note, we buried his ashes at our horse's field which was one of his favourite places to go.

We now also have another brother for Rox who was really missing him, a lovely Saluki/Greyhound called Zeuk, they are all different and Strider is still missed every day. Zeuk is not a replacement at all, but cheers us up and we think Strider would be pleased he is here, he loved other dogs and if it hadn't been for him we wouldn't have Zeuk who was a rescue boy.

RIP Strider 24/7/2012

He had just turned nine at the beginning of the June before he sadly died.

We love you Strider ♥

Bobby, Gucci and Lucky
By
Rebekah Wood

Bobby was the first black cat to adopt me when he was about two years old. Sadly, he was run over two years later.

In July that year Lucky (aged nine months) adopted me and the following year my husband sadly died. Lucky gave me so much comfort during that time. About three years later I wrote my first book 'A Cat's Tale' about Bobby & Lucky. A year later my daughter purchased Gucci, a beautiful Turkish angora kitten, from the pet shop. Tragically Gucci was run over and we had to have her put to sleep.

About five years ago, we were adopted by Bobby II, & sadly he too was claimed by the road. On 10th May 2015 Lucky crossed the rainbow bridge after sixteen precious years with me, which as you can imagine was really hard to deal with. I am at present, cat-less, but I know one day they will all find me when the time is right.

Over the years my beautiful cats have given me much comfort, joy and friendship. They have been there for me in my darkest moments and I feel their presence around me still.

I feel sure Joanne's book will bring much comfort to those who have lost their cherished fur babies.

I love you Bobby, Gucci and Lucky ♥

Kiwi

By

Shannon Cordray

This is a tough story to tell. I had Kiwi for eight years. She was a testing dog on so many levels. She would run away constantly, didn't listen, and peed on the carpet, not to mention the barking nonstop.

When I got divorced, I left her with my ex husband because he had the yard and house that she was used to. She and I at this point were not friends.

Four years went by and my ex husband got married again. My ex and his wife had two big Labradors, but unfortunately they started attacking Kiwi when no one was home and finally my ex husband was faced with the choice of putting her down or letting me have her as she wasn't exactly able to be re-homed due to her naughty behaviour. And of course, regardless of our differences, I took her back.

By then, she was quite hard of hearing, slow, and old. I fell totally in love with her and I promised to love her and take care of her till the end. We had finally renewed our relationship and I was going to stick it out with her no matter what!

She was incontinent and oh so stubborn, but I loved every second I had with her. Trying to make up for the animosity we had before. I knew she understood. We had made a pact, and I wasn't going to let her down.

A couple years later, my son was in college. My kids and I were staying with our grandma to help her out in her final days. I asked my mother to watch Kiwi for me while as I was away to visit my son in Athens, so that my grandma would not be burdened by taking care of her. When I came home, my mother informed me that she had put Kiwi down! Yes, put to sleep! Stating that she was hurt and that she had no other choice, since I was out of town. I immediately called the vet that put her down and he informed me that Kiwi was not hurt in any way and that my mother claimed she had cancer and could not take care of "her" dog anymore and so requested this was her only choice. Needless to say, I was devastated, and I still am to be perfectly honest, how could my mum do this to me and how could I have lost her after everything. I miss her every day and think of her often.

I still feel much guilt that the promise I made her was broken and that I was not able to be with her in the end. This is a terrible story, I know. I loved this dog with my whole heart and I am so sorry that I could not be there for her until the end. Maybe sometimes life gives you a lesson to learn from, I'm quite sure this was one of those times. I truly believe her spirit is with me now, and hopefully she forgives me.

I love you Kiwi ♥

Topcat
By
Michelle Merritt

Topcat, who we always called TC, was nineteen and a half years old when he passed in Oct 2014.

He was a stray kitten that arrived one day and never left! TC had a lot of health problems but still had a long and happy life. In his last year, he developed a tumour which was in-operable and ultimately his kidneys began to fail. Letting him go was the hardest decision our family have had to make, but TC let us know when the time was right and we know he's gone to a better place and is now at peace. He was such a wonderful, intelligent cat who brought a great deal of joy to our family.

He is greatly missed by all of us including our dog, his friend Max.

We love you Topcat ♥

Hal

By

Martha Brindley

My dog was Hal, a little rescue Whippet; he was from Greyhound Awareness League.

He was ten years old when he passed peacefully at home. He had both myself by his side and Sam, my other Whippet. I rescued Hal when he was twelve weeks old. I fell in love with his cheeky personality and the bond between us was still strong ten years later. He truly was a remarkable boy, so beautiful and full of love and loyalty.

Hal and I participated in agility and had great fun competing! We never won anything but always raised smiles from the crowd, which gave us more pleasure than a rosette any day!

Hal went on to be a Therapet and a Blue Cross education dog, teaching children safe approach to dogs. He was so gentle and kind and loved all the children.

I took Hal all over the country with me on various holidays from South Uist to Wales and in between.

He was my loyal companion for ten years and had separation anxiety if I had to leave him. Sadly, Hal had autoimmune disease at four years old and I nursed him back to health for eighteen months.

He survived for another six years but in April 2014, my vet came to my house and Hal was very sadly put to sleep peacefully in my arms.

He was the most delightful and loyal little boy and I still miss him very much. I always take comfort from knowing I gave him a wonderful life and he brought such pleasure to everyone he met.

I love you Hal ♥

Simba

By

Lena Diana

My beloved Simba was a loving, affectionate soul. He was born 3/2/97 and gave me love and comfort for sixteen wonderful years.

I made the heartbreaking decision everyone dreads to let him cross the bridge on 7/10/13.
He was so loved and he always knew how to comfort me in my darkest times.

For anyone who has a loving pet in their lives, it is such a blessing, and making that decision to let them go is so heartbreaking. But know that they will always be in your heart and the memories you have of them will make it that much easier until you see them again across the bridge.

I love you Simba ♥

Dino and Zara

By

Voula Kantarzoglou

DINO: I remember the first day I laid eyes on who became the greatest love of my life, my precious boy Dino! I went to visit friends of mine which were looking after him for someone else. I walked out into the backyard and there he was, up on an elevated piece of land behind a metal railing. I will never forget the first glance as we spotted each other! It was a long stare with a sense of breathlessness and there it was instantly! LOVE AT FIRST SIGHT The love connection was exactly what we all hear about it! I was completely mesmerised and I knew the feeling was mutual! Dino started to cry and jump around like crazy, wanting me to approach him! I went to meet him with amazement and he attached himself to me and wouldn't leave my side. It was like we had known each other for ever. Our souls reconnected! I knew right at that moment that I had been chosen as his! We knew right then that we had to be together!

Dino taught me the true meaning of unconditional love! He was my whole world and I was his!

He was my best friend, my protector, my companion, my child, my strength and hope! He was my own private blessing and miracle! He taught me what it is to love and to be loved and accepted for
Who you are without expectations or judgements!

He was a comedian and constantly made me smile! He taught me what it is to be selfless and how to put the one you love and their needs above your own! I loved him with every cell of my being as we were each other's everything! The way he stared into my eyes and waited for my every move so he could be by my side was incredible! At times, it felt like I had a tail attached! When it was bed time he would come and nudge me and cry to get me to go to bed, as he wouldn't go without me. He was such a charmer especially with the ladies of both the human and dog species! Everyone would comment on how handsome he was which of course made me so proud!

Dino had been fighting several diseases for the last four years and a few months after he was given the all clear, his specialist discovered an incurable and inoperable tumour! I have no words to describe the horror and desperation and despair that took over my world!

After a four year battle that graced him the doctors' title of "Miracle Dog" because he had fought hard and won to everyone's disbelief. However later on, this was to be a battle that was not going to be won. It was back! I was completely, totally and utterly devastated beyond words! I was in total disbelief and could not accept defeat and that I was going to lose the love of my life and baby! We had tried everything known to man and medicine! I was told it was a matter of time! Hearing those words I felt I could hardly breathe I was so devastated. I was nauseous at the idea of losing him! I didn't know how I would be able to make this decision or when and how I would know that it is time. His specialist told me that Dino will let me know when it is time.

That sounded non-understandable to me, but just as he said, I got Dino's message, it was very clear and I knew my boy could no longer take the pain.

That morning I called his specialist, it had been only five weeks since diagnosis.

My worst fear had come! Just like that, my whole world fell apart! My greatest love was gone and I was all alone and devastated! I was in total shock and disbelief! The reason I got out of bed every morning had gone! I had all this love inside but with no one to give it to! I fell into deep loss and grief and couldn't function. I spent one month in bed only crying and sleeping as much as possible to not be in touch with reality! I honestly thought I was never going to recover and a part of me never has. I reached out to a pet loss grief counsellor for advice and the thing that he said that helped make any sense to me was 'grief is an expression of love' somehow those words did something that enabled me to get up a step at a time.

One of the things that I will always remember about my precious boy Dino is, how when he was really begging for something for example a walk he would say; "Mum" with such a complaint in his expression and I would reply "don't you mum me". That one little word would make my whole soul smile and it still does, every time I recall this loving memory!

My only advice is that time doesn't heal anything when it comes to the loss of a loved one, but we learn how to live without them!

If I could tell my Dino one thing it would be "I love you more than words can express and I always will!" I would repeatedly tell him "I love you immensely and endlessly! You will be forever in my heart and thoughts and I miss you every single day! Not a single day passes that I don't think of you!

Thank you for the love and lessons you taught me and thank you for the blessing you brought to my life with having had you in it!"

I love you Dino ♥

Rosie

By

Beverley Conlon Bradshaw

My beautiful Rosie, aged seven years and six months when she passed, she sadly had a well known Westie lung disease.

Rosie was my world, she wasn't just a dog, but my companion and best friend, she was spoilt and took advantage of that, she knew when I was down or poorly and didn't want to leave my side. I laughed with her, cried with her, talked all the time to her, as I still do after nearly four years of her passing. My heart will never mend, but now I begin to think about the good things we had and how lucky I was to have her with me, I will never forget her.

I love you Rosie ♥.

Gracie

By

Dawn Simpson

I received a phone call from my friend Margaret to see if I could help a friend of hers to get her dogs ready, they were to be re-homed As they were not used to being handled by strangers Margaret thought I would be the right person to help. So, it was arranged, I was to meet them and it went like this.............

This was when I met Lynda for the first time, she had heard I was good with animals with my healing and I could maybe get some of hers settled and trusted in me enough to help place them with their new families without all the stress that normally occurs.

So, I was introduced to some gorgeous Golden Retrievers, one at a time and I worked with them, only giving what they wanted as they asked, the two girls loved head massage, so sweet, it followed on to a full body massage with a little bit of reiki thrown in. Both of them were very unsure at the beginning, but were happy to feel able to ask for what they needed. Then Lynda asked me if her son could bring Gracie down too, Gracie was another Golden Retriever. From where I was sitting I could see straight into the garden. This beautiful albeit small Golden Retriever was let out of her kennel for a pee, she wasn't facing me, but was side on, she turned her head and ran full pelt across the garden, down the steps then straight into the sitting room and put her head straight onto my lap. She was looking up at me with these soulful eyes, connecting like we knew each other but we had never met before. I looked at Lynda and Margaret, they both had their mouths wide open in shock. Margaret laughed and said "I will tell you later Dawn". Gracie looked over at Lynda with a guilty look and went over, placing her head so gently on her lap and looked at her. Lynda said to Gracie that she was more than happy with this and to go back to me if she wanted to. Lynda went into the kitchen to make a cuppa but I know it was to give Gracie space. Gracie wanted me to touch her face, and then continue all over her until I ended up bent right over her and couldn't do any more as I couldn't reach. So, I sat on the floor and spread my legs like you would for a child and asked if she wanted to come in and I can do more for her. She did, Margaret couldn't believe it, and her expression said it all.

On the way home Margaret told me about Gracie's life. She was born and connected with Louise, her first mum, Lynda's daughter who sadly passed away with cancer.

Lynda sadly now also had cancer and was getting her family ready and safe before her time came to go, it was a devastating story and we both had tears rolling down our faces and our hearts hurt so bad knowing the situation that Lynda was facing with her devoted dogs, especially Gracie. I can't forget that day, the day of re-homing; it was like a clear video in my head.

Gracie was a shell, wouldn't talk or even look at anyone apart from her immediate family, there was a huge worry for her future. I felt so honoured, when she chose us, that is myself and Saffie, my other dog for her new family with Lynda's approval.

Gracie has given me more than words can write, she has given me belief, she has touched so many lives in the two years she was physically with me and was looked after fondly by everyone she met, Saffie her saluki 'sister' was always supporting and guiding her, it was like they always had that relationship forever but it was from the very first meeting. Gracie shared her love and hugged everyone who loved her. She had no hang ups, took those on face value, always wanting to heal those in pain, or illness. We went and visited Lynda in the hospice and both Gracie and Saffie took me straight to her room, we had never been there before, it was so surreal but humbling. Soon after Lynda sadly passed

It was a gorgeous day, well for us here in a grey raining Scotland. We were at our usual walk for the first walk of the day, I had met up with Jess my daughter who was going on to her work (vet nurse) and took Morgen (Jess's Australian shepherd) and Saffie and Gracie who were all thoroughly enjoying themselves. It was as we were ending the walk and I was just about to call them to get leads on, when Gracie looked at me; it was like someone punching me in my heart. Gracie told me she was dying.

I didn't want to believe her, she didn't look different, her coat, skin, everything was normal but her movement had changed enough for me to know she was meaning it.

I rushed to the vets, Jess couldn't understand why I was there and said Gracie will be fine, she is just slightly off. I insisted her bloods etc were taken. We had to wait two long weeks to do bloods again, they were not right. And the devastating news came, it was leukaemia and it was bad!

Gracie wasn't expected to make the weekend. So, we had fun that weekend, went to a big agricultural show, fed her with full roast chickens and any other delicious foods she usually loved. She was happy! We were pumping her full of steroids to keep her appetite up. I really think she knew what was happening and seemed to enjoy how things were going; we even met and spent the day with her lovely vet Emma which I know helped us through such a hard heartbreaking time. It was Emma who helped her pass over. It was so beautiful but so heartbreaking for all of us, we all struggled. But Gracie didn't, but then again, she knew. I miss her being here but Saffie, well she is still struggling with her soul mate not being here anymore. The loneliness and grief in her eyes is what I find hard to watch to be honest. I watched it with Gracie; she had lost both her human mums, and both to cancer, and sadly, both in a very short time. Gracie was full of love and those precious to her passed over and then for her to go with cancer too, what a life to have had for one so young, just turned six. I always knew there was something different with Gracie, but I didn't realise she was ill all the time we had her, but I believe Saffie knew and that was why she always cared for her so differently.

Too many people think animals don't feel loss and grieve like we do, but they do. I see it so much, I watch it in Saffie every day, only sometimes while she is occupied with her pups do you see a bit of a change, but then she feels sad again, her eyes tell me hauntingly.

I know and accept it will take time for her to accept the loss, just like us humans, but we all have that love, our hearts feel the same. So, I talk about Gracie and Laugh with Saffie so she can heal too, it helps me as well. We feel the same. I have experienced so much while Gracie has been with us that my life has taken a different path, so I say 'Thank you Gracie'. Through our time with her, we have learnt so much and now have another chapter in our lives just starting, much of it is owed to having Lynda and Gracie in my, or should I say our lives.

Even though it was for only two years, it feels like forever. I am honoured, truly honoured. So, here's looking forward to the future, thanks Gracie.

I love you ♥

Cassie & Sami
By
Lyn Edmonds

I was lucky enough to share my life with my rough collie girl Cassie, she was my baby. She would also mother everything including the children. I still miss and love her although she's been gone four years now, she lived to be seventeen and sadly had to be put to sleep with heart trouble. My border collie girl Sami, who we lost last year aged fifteen, had two strokes the last causing a haemorrhage, she was a wonderfully loyal girl who went everywhere with me in the car. She loved being driven around in the car!

I love and miss them both and hope we'll be together one day.

I love you both ♥

Poppy
By
Kerry Wisbey

This is the story of how I rescued Poppy, a wonderful little sparrow who fulfilled and changed my life more than I could realize, and who also lived to the great age of eighteen!

I believe it was in the summertime: I was working in the garden with my parents when we heard a scuffle, and then the screech of a bird. We have a lot of birds in our garden who squabble, but this was different. We went down the side of the house to check, and we found, laying on our side step, a tiny little sparrow. She was barely moving and breathing. We couldn't believe she had fallen all the way from the top of our two-storey house! My Dad picked her up gently and we took her inside the house, she had a big lump on her chest and couldn't lift her head. I put one of my huge bed socks tucked in half and I sat her in that as it was a cocoon for her and kept her warm.

I wasn't sure what to feed her, so I broke up some bread and covered it with hot water and some milk, then using some tweezers. I fed her as best as I could and she did take it very well. I kept her in my bedroom, on my desk near the radiator, so she could keep warm in her little cocoon sock bed. It was on the same day that we took her to a local lady who helps injured birds and other animals recover. She examined Poppy and said that she had a lump on her chest from the fall, which had to be drained but it would be risky. By this time, Poppy was getting worse; she was still eating but was quite weak. I stepped out of the lady's shed while she did the procedure on Poppy with my Dad holding her. We took Poppy home with the lady telling us the next forty-eight hours would be crucial: Poppy would either live or she would die from the injury or the shock. So, for forty-eight hours she stayed on my desk beside my bed and I fed her every hour with the bread and milk, even through the night.

The next morning there was a slight improvement with her, she was able to get out of the bed, but she was still very weak. I continued to feed her every hour through the day and the night again. I was praying she would be all right. I woke the next morning to find that she was hopping around the floor, actually asking for food. I was thrilled! I knew she was still too weak to be let out, and not fully recovered, so I made her a little box with an opening which I tied onto a perch. This became her tree house! I also made her a platform to stand on, as she hadn't yet got used to standing on a perch. Poppy loved her tree house, and stayed in it most of the time. During the next week, she got stronger and stronger. We let her out of the cage a few times to test her flying and mobility and she would sit on my Dad's shoulder and pull his hair.

But her favourite game was playing with his earring which hung down, she used to pull on it until he shouted, it was very funny.

Poppy did fly, but I think because she fell very hard it must have affected her balance because she always flew in circles and crashed into things. We kept letting her out to practice in case it was a one-off thing, but after a few more weeks we realized it was permanent, so unfortunately she could never be released outside because she wouldn't survive and we didn't want one of the local cats to get her. So, Poppy the sparrow became a permanent member of the family. Poppy continued to grow and ended up only coming to my room at night for bed, sleeping on my desk beside me. She did get cross when I moved under my duvet, she would try and peck me because I woke her up! During the day, I carried her cage downstairs and she sat on the windowsill watching the other birds from her cozy tree house.

Every morning and evening I would feed Poppy the bread and milk with tweezers, and during the day she used to eat a broken-up piece of malted milk biscuit and bread which she would either eat dry or wet, as she had learned to dip them in her water pot. If I was pottering about the house doing different things I would put the radio on and Poppy would sing to it from her tree house, it always made me and my family smile when we heard Poppy singing. She also got into some mischief as she sat on the windowsill she would stand on her fat ball on the platform and grab Mum's net curtain and pull it through into her cage and cover it with sand. Then, before bed, she would come out to cause mischief for an hour or so then come back up to bed with me.

Poppy lasted an amazing eighteen years, and was very much a part of the family. She had moments when she was poorly so she was never 100%, but towards the end of her time with us, her breathing became heavy and when we heard a rattle, we knew she wouldn't be with us very much longer. I had a feeling one evening it was her time to go, I had been talking to Poppy (I used to talk to her a lot about anything really if I was upset or worried, and she seemed to listen and would tweet back) I decided that I would take her up to my room that night (as she had stopped coming up, because we had another bird in the lounge and they seemed to keep each other company) but I thought it was the night so I took her up with me. I sat her on my desk and made sure she was facing me so that I could keep an eye on her. I fell asleep but I was woken in the night by the sound of Poppy's breathing. I sat up, put the light on, and found she was lying on the floor gasping with a terrible rattle. I got upset as I didn't want my dear friend Poppy to go. I told her to hold on, but she looked at me and in her eyes I could see she was in pain and it was time for her. I was crying and was very sad, I stroked her and told my wonderful friend of eighteen years that it was all right to go and that I would manage, I would miss her terribly but she could go. Poppy surprised me by jumping up onto my hand and laid on it as she passed away. I laid her in her tree house and woke my Mum up; she helped me make a bed for Poppy, a little sheet for her to lie on, a blanket and a cushion. She just looked as if she'd gone to bed. It was sweet. The next day we put Poppy and her bed into a small box and buried her in the garden, and I made a Cross to have her name on. We were all very sad and even writing this now makes me sad.

Poppy was very much part of our family and she is very much missed, but our memories of her are forever. I was very lucky to know her and have her as a friend, and I will treasure my memories of my little friend Poppy forever.

I love you Poppy ♥

Wild Geese

By

Ricky Martin

This is Wild Geese and I at the stables where he is looking for more mints!

I'm in a racing syndicate and Geese was a much loved horse with a lovely personality. He was only eight years old when he passed over. He had been recuperating well from a leg injury and so had been enjoying life in the fields with his friends.

'Geese' unfortunately passed over, he was truly my favourite horse and will be very sadly missed.

I love you Wild Geese.

Bir-Bird
By
Shirlyn

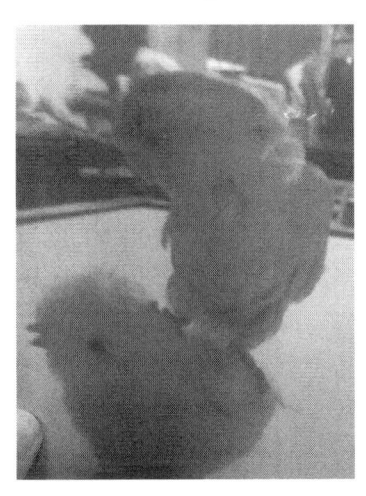

Until now every time I wanted to share my story with someone, I held back, I am scared that it won't be taken seriously; I mean it's a difficult topic to talk about, that is, until I was asked to contribute to this book. I just didn't want anyone thinking I was making it up or to be judged. But you see, I believe it as it is. I had a pet bird, he was a Love bird, Love birds usually come in pairs, but mine was single. We called him Bir-Bird. His wing feathers were trimmed shorter by my uncle who previously owned him, so Bir-Bird couldn't fly, and so I was always able to take him out of his cage to play with him, which he loved Some birds which are pets are always caged or chained/tied to somewhere and people hardly have close connection with them which I think is so sad. But with Bir-Bird and I it was different. Bir-Bird was a very wary bird, always ready to peck whenever something went near him.

He'd also peck at my family members, but not me. He was usually calm with me. When I stuck my hand to bring him out of the cage to play, Bir-Bird would always pose just as I pointed my phone camera at him, he loved me taking pictures of him. He was a real show off. He would do his silly bird dance when I played catchy songs, he was so funny and a true character.

I had Bir-Bird for three years before he died in September 2012 it's been so long now and I'm still close to tearing up writing this to you today, I cried so much when he died, it was so sad. Not long after my dad flushed his body down the toilet bowl (I know, I was so sad about it) something odd happened. You see you only normally see terrapins in pet shops in my area. And one day when my friend came to my house, she brought in a terrapin and told me that the terrapin was found walking towards her when she was walking under my block. She claimed that the terrapin told her (she could communicate with spirits) that he was Bir-Bird and he came back as a terrapin to look for me. I was doubtful at first but like I told you, you only see terrapins in pet shops here. There is no way you can just randomly spot one anywhere! And this particular one was spotted right under my block, walking towards my friend when she was making her way to my house. Coincidence? I don't think so! Plus, this terrapin sometimes responds when I call for Bir-Bird, and it's the only terrapin I have personally ever known that won't retreat back into its shell when I pet its head.

Unfortunately, one day my terrapins went missing. It turned out someone at home released all of them into the river beside my block, as you can imagine I was totally devastated, because yet again I believed I had lost Bir-Bird all over again.

It's been a long time since I last saw Bir-Bird and sometimes I wonder where he is and how he's doing.

He was my best friend and would always have a place in my heart

I hope he knows I am so sorry that I failed him as a carer and that I love him so dearly. And where ever he is in whatever form I hope he is safe and happy. He was the best pet I could ever have.

I love you Bir-Bird ♥

Jasper

By

Amanda Miller

I wasn't looking for a naughty ginger cat. I'd never lived with a ginger cat, so didn't know about their infamous reputation for mischief. My husband Dave and I had gone to see a litter of British shorthair kittens, in the breeder's home. Our previous Himalayan cat had been put to sleep two months earlier, and we were missing having a cat around. Having chosen a blue female kitten (quiet, affectionate, and sleepy), we were sorting out the paperwork when I spotted this very small ball of orange stalking behind the furniture.

He was too cute not to scoop up for a cuddle, which he protested about! Turns out he was a mishap! He was a litter of one, and was his mother's first pregnancy. There had been no intention to breed her, but her sire had sought her out.

The ginger kittens' mother had mated with her own father. What an incestuous start to his life. It turns out that at that point in time he was only five weeks old, so wouldn't be ready to leave at the same time as the other kitten. It gave me time to talk Dave into letting me have both them both. Fast forward another six weeks. Our blue kitten, who we named Misty, had settled quietly into life with us. She liked to sleep, and never caused any fuss.

On the day that I went to collect Jasper (with the intention at that point of naming him Dylan) the breeder told me that his mum would probably be pleased to get some peace in her life. He had been very boisterous and demanding, and having no siblings, he pestered mum instead. Note that she didn't tell me this until I had paid for him. She also told me that I shouldn't insult him by calling him 'ginger'. Apparently, he was a show quality red tabby! On the fifteen minute car journey home, he was very vocal. It was at that point that he just didn't seem to suit the name Dylan. Jasper was the name that occurred to me on that drive home. *'Jasper Carrot.'* Well, he was ginger! Misty, Dave and I spent the next few months regretting having to live with Jasper.

From his first night at home he was noisy if he couldn't barge his way into our bedroom. He had ripped up the hallway carpet outside any doors that were closed to him. He jumped onto everything. He wouldn't use the litter tray, preferring to leave us a daily offering next to the tray instead, earning him an early nickname of "little sh*t". He fought his way out of the velvet collar I put on him (it lasted less than 24 hours) and he tormented Misty into playing with him rather than sleeping. He was so boisterous that we chose to have him neutered as soon as he was old enough – we really didn't want him to discover the joys of spraying his territory too. When I went to pick him up after surgery, the vet said he would probably be sleepy for the next day or so.

Not a chance. Although both he and Misty were predominantly housecats, it was a very warm evening, and as our house was on a quiet cul-de-sac, we did let them into the back garden when the weather was good. Normally just before their regular dinner time of six o'clock. On the night in question there was an ominous quiet outside, and no one demanding dinner. Further investigation revealed that they had discovered a hedgehog. They were just being inquisitive, and had not caused the poor thing any injury, but my first thought was "fleas"! Both cats were immediately impounded in the kitchen and checked over. Thankfully we escaped from an infestation. By the time we had the cats for seven months or so, we moved house, due to Dave's company being relocated. It was the Friday of the August bank holiday, 2011. We moved from Kent to the West Midlands.

On the day of the move, we kept both cats with a litter tray, food and water in the bathroom (removal men do not need to go into the main bathroom, so it was safe and secure). This meant that by the time the house was empty, cats were a little agitated. Dave was doing the 120 miles in one car with the cats, and I was following on with my car, my mum and the vacuum cleaner once we had tidied up, so we left a little later. Dave phoned not long after leaving, being on the M25. I could hear Jasper protesting loudly over the phone. He kept it up for the entire journey. Misty by contrast was (and still is) a very quiet cat. By the time I finally found our new house (this was in the days before sat-navs were widely available) Dave and the removal van were waiting.

Again, the cats got to inhabit the (new) bathroom, so once the removers had unloaded everything, we allowed the cats out. Mum and I left to try to locate a local supermarket, leaving Dave to open the loft hatch and put some things out of the way. It was a hot day, so at one point when we were out, Dave stopped to sit in the garden with a cold drink.

He was wise enough to leave the cats inside, but not wise enough to the workings of the mind of a ginger tom. Jasper had to check out all the new places, so having a complete new house wasn't enough. Dave had left the step ladder underneath the open loft hatch.

When I returned with the shopping, Dave was trying to reach Jasper. Jasper was behind the cold water tank. Building a bed in the fibre glass loft insulation! He was beyond arm's length in the un-boarded loft. We thought that if we left him there for a little while he would get himself out. After a couple of hours, still no sign of him. It was hot in the loft. I started to worry about the heat and the fiberglass. So, Dave goes back up with a broom. He managed to prod him out from his spot behind the tank, and grab him by the scruff of his neck. Then try to pass him through the (quite small) loft hatch down for me to catch. That was the plan. Somehow cats know how to lengthen their legs and stick each out at awkward angles so that they will not fit through the gaps (just like trying to get one into their carrier for a trip to the vets). In the end, Dave just had to let go of him and drop him down. Jasper was hot, and covered in fiberglass, so he needed to have a bath. So, the first bath time in our new house involved Jaspers one and only experience was in the kitchen sink, being held in a plastic laundry basket, with my shampoo! What a long day.

    A little more than a year later we were on the move again, a temporary job assignment in the USA. Both cat's needs to get a pet passport within a month of them being introduced.

    On the morning that the cats needed to go to Heathrow, Jasper managed one of his disappearing tricks. He wasn't going near that extra-large carrier that had appeared in the hallway. I had kept all doors and windows closed but could not find his hiding place.

I opened the sliding patio door in the kitchen; he could never resist seeing what was happening. He heard the familiar sound, and his little orange face popped up from the top of the cooker hood. How had he gotten himself up there? And how did he know that it would be a great hiding place? Fast forward two and a half years, and we needed to come back home.

If my UK vet didn't understand the pet passport scheme, my US vet knew even less. I learned a lot about the UK quarantine requirements within a short space of time. Put simply, quarantine starts from the time of the blood test for rabies. We had to fly home three months after the test. Meaning we were three months short of the six months quarantine period. Our babies had to spend three months in quarantine before we could bring them home. At least there is a quarantine kennels near Birmingham airport, so I could visit every other day.

Jasper seemed to become institutionalized in the 4x6 cubicle that he shared with Misty. They both slept a lot, and were not very interested when I went to see them. Not like Jasper's normal wall-climbing self. They both put on quite a bit of weight. When we finally brought them home, three years since they had last been in the house, Jasper went straight to one of his favourite places in the airing cupboard. He hadn't forgotten how he could annoy us by rattling the cupboard door for long enough that we would end up opening it, allowing him to snuggle down amongst the towels. Then he got us trained enough so that we didn't ever fully shut the door, and he could open in by putting his paw into the gap.

His absolute favourite spot was in the bay window in the lounge. He was very nosey, so liked to watch what was happening at the end of our drive. He must have been immensely patient, as very little happened!

But there was always a little ginger face looking out for us whenever we came home.

There was also always a lot of ginger hair over my blinds, so much so that I replaced my cream vertical blinds with orange roman blinds. Jasper had dictated our colour scheme.

It's still really poignant for me to write this, in the week before Christmas 2016. This is the first Christmas without him. It would also have been his birthday on the 14th. In spring 2015, we noticed that he was sneezing a lot.

We took him to the vet, who found that he had some dental issues, and that by removing the relevant teeth, it might affect pressure in his sinuses. That seemed to solve the problem for a couple of months, then the sneezing returned. We were prescribed a number of different medications, but nothing made the sneezing go away, and he also developed a persistent runny left eye.

During one of the many visits back to the vet, and noticing that his weight was decreasing at each weigh-in, the vet suggested that he went for some investigative work, and she made a referral. I remember the drive to the centre, with him in his carrier on the passenger seat of the car. He was rather quiet. I had to leave him for blood tests and an endoscope in the nostrils which required a general anaesthetic.

Having lost a dog some years ago under anaesthetic just for some routine tests, I was anxious. But I also believed that naughty, lively Jasper would be invincible.

It turned out that he had a lymphoma in his nostril. Diagnosis was not good, and we could treat him with chemotherapy and radiotherapy, but there was no guarantee. He was fifteen years old, and I would not put him through that to prolong his life for maybe a few more weeks. The Vet said he might have anywhere between six months and a couple of years.

Palliative care it would be, and he would be completely spoiled in that time. Dreamies cat treats and raw chicken on demand! Getting him home, it was hard to believe there was anything wrong with him. The only outward signs were his runny eye and also his nostril that had joined in. He still had a big appetite and could hear the removal of the carving knife from the knife block from the other side of the house. When it came to begging for raw chicken, he could teach a dog a few things! We had regular prescriptions from the vet for medications to help any bacterial infection and steroids to help his body deal with the lymphoma. His regular weigh-ins showed a constant decline.

He has lost 50% of his body weight, and looked like an old cat now. It all happened during the week of the summer solstice. He had stopped jumping up onto the window sill, and instead would get there via the arm of the sofa, which was lower. He stopped sitting up and watching out of the window, and instead laid down and slept there. He didn't announce his presence in the early morning, both vocally and by launching himself onto the bed. He stopped purring. I remember kneeling on the lawn on the actual evening of the solstice, watching the sun go down over the garden. He trotted up to me and stood on my legs. This was the last time he came to me. I stroked him and talked to him, and I think it was his way of saying goodbye. That final weekend he didn't go upstairs at all.

We have hard floors downstairs, with carpet only in the lounge. We began to leave the lounge door open so that he could sleep on the sofas in there. He didn't, he chose to sleep on the rug. It was as if he could no longer jump up. He turned his head away from any form of petting. I called the vet, and discussed his behavior. It seemed to be the right time. But I wanted another day. I don't work on Mondays, so was there to observe him. He went out into the garden once and sat looking into the flower bed.

He kept his back to the house, as if he was saying goodbye. It began to rain, so I called to him before closing the kitchen door. He didn't move. I left it a few minutes and the rain got heavier. He didn't move. On the third time of calling, he slowly walked under one of the evergreen shrubs. Only when the rain became even heavier did he come in when I opened the door again. He was drenched. I'd never known him to allow himself to get that wet, and it was the only time I had to towel dry him. He spent the rest of the day on the rug, but not in a comfortable position. He was struggling to breathe.

I had been a member of a Facebook group called "The Ginger Cat Appreciation Society", and had posted a little about Jasper's situation.

One of the most helpful comments was that "you are not prolonging his life; you are just prolonging his death". That helped me to decide. I booked the final appointment for the next evening, after work. It is only a ten minute walk to the vets, or a ninety second drive, but walking on that final journey was not an option. I needed Dave to come with me, as I wouldn't be able to drive back.

When I got home, there was no ginger face waiting for me. Part of me hoped that maybe he had gone peacefully. But he was still on the rug in the lounge. I tried to stroke his head but he turned away from me. He wasn't enjoying life any more. Maybe the hardest part for any of us during the final visit is the feeling of betrayal when bringing out the carrier for the last time. I thought that I could just bring it to him and scoop him in. No. He actually got up and ran up the stairs. He hadn't been upstairs for several days. He ran under the bed, then back downstairs again, where Dave picked him up. I felt so wretched. It was raining. I was so relieved that it was not a bright sunny day. The words of the 1970's song 'Seasons in the Sun' had been in my head all day;

*'Goodbye my friend, it's hard to die
When all the birds are singing in the sky
Now that the spring is in the air....'*

He was silent on the short journey. He didn't get out of the carrier. It was as if he had given up. It is a canvas style carrier, with a removable bottom pad. The vet took the bottom out. He still did not move. She did a quick assessment and confirmed that sadly the time had come. I stroked between his ears for the duration. He didn't move at all. I only knew it was finally over when the vet confirmed that his heart had stopped.

    The last I ever saw of him was when she carried him out. We were going to had him cremated.
Less than 10 minutes later we were back home. There was one less of us. I sat down on the bottom stair to take my shoes off, and cried. I sobbed for a long time. Looking back, the advantage of crying is that you don't have time to think beyond the present moment of trying to breathe. I got through a lot of tissues that night. And it still rained. I went to work the next morning, which helped a great deal. It's a very small company, with only five of us. And everyone else had also lost a pet within the last couple of years. In some ways, it really helped to talk to those who just know how it feels. And I didn't break down in the office! I would say that for the first week I kept thinking that 'at this time last week he was still here.'

    I get a reminder every month as it fell on pay day. This month will be the six month anniversary. I have passed (recently) through his 16th birthday without any melancholy. But I think that was because I had recently put up the Christmas tree, so had already reflected on all the times he had been there to nose around underneath it. For a cheeky cat, he never caused any damage to it. He did sometimes curl up and make himself comfortable amongst the presents.

Jaspers ashes live in a bronze casket shaped like a sleeping cat. It lives on the window sill where he spent so much time watching. Each day when I open the blinds I stroke it. He is still here in his favourite spot.

On the first day that it was placed there, Misty climbed onto the window sill and sat next to it. She had never sat on that side of the windowsill before, and hasn't done so since. They had an agreement as to which side was his, and which side was hers. Jasper had always made us laugh when he was alive.

One summer afternoon when living in Massachusetts, Jasper proudly walked in with a chipmunk. "Jasper, put that down" I yelled. So he did. It wasn't injured in any way, and they are not called ground squirrels for nothing.

The chipmunk sprinted into the floor level (called base boards in America) heating system. It stayed there for around six hours. It is not easy removing a chipmunk from an open plan house, whilst also keeping two very interested cats out of the way.

I also have a keen interest in numerology. I recently found his pedigree certificate. He was born on 14/12/2000. If you add all those numbers together then come to 10. That reduces to 1. Also the first letter on the alphabet is 1. The 10th is J. The 19th (1=9=10) is S. And I decided that Jasper suited him better than Dylan! I have several books on numerology, but only one of them refers to pets:"If your pet is a 1, be prepared to be amazed. This animal will forever choose the opposite of what you offer, sleep in bizarre places, show incredible independence and determination and perhaps allow you to become his friend. This pet also displays a dazzling sense of humor." *Titania Hardy – Zillions.*

My advice for those who have suffered loss would be to have them cremated rather than buried, so that you can have some physical part of them with you.

The fact that I was also recommended a manufacturer of caskets specifically for cats means that he is still part of our living room decor. And if I could say one thing to Jasper, it would be to remind him of how much he made us laugh.

Thank you for teaching us so much about cat intellect and character. And yes, we always knew that the payback for having you for so many years would always be the grief at the end. You were a price worth paying.

I love you Jasper! ♥

Basil

By

Brimble Wharton

We had a terrible time during the New Year period of 2000. My husband had just lost his dear father, and then our beautiful dog Papi, a handsome Beauceron X German Shepherd (who had travelled with us just like Asterix our horse) to different places in France, then moving to England, was tragically killed on a nearby quarry train line. My husband Simon had been through so much heartbreak. Papi had been his dog, and the double tragedy felt very cruel indeed. He had been a shepherd for many years, and had always had sheepdogs. They had been his very close companions.

By the middle of the summer, Simon's birthday was approaching, and I knew I secretly wanted to get him a dog.

He had said he didn't want another, but I knew his life would never be complete until he had that canine bond again. I saw the litter of Border Collie puppies advertised at my local farming cooperative, and I felt very drawn to the advertisement. I made enquiries and went along to see them. They were from very well bred parents, both whom could be seen. The father was a proper working collie, and the owners were very experienced. Most of the puppies had been taken. I was on my own and knew I was taking a risk, choosing Simon's next potential soul mate. There were two or maybe three left, I honestly can't remember, because I was instantly drawn to Basil! Another person had previously reserved him, a gentleman confined to a wheelchair, and Basil had apparently wanted very much to curl up on his lap. This however fell through, and Basil was still up for sale. He was the most gorgeous black and white bundle, plump, inquisitive, and very fluffy!

A couple of weeks later, it was Simon's birthday. I disappeared off to secretly collect Basil in the car, and then complete with big red ribbon, I presented him to Simon. It was love at first sight! Basil grew into an amazing dog. Our eldest child was still a baby, and from the very start Basil was 110% loving and trustworthy around him and our other three children that arrived later were equally cherished by Basil. He was so gentle and kind. He was never angry or jealous, nor was he in any way domineering.

He simply loved being around family and people in general. Simon very sadly lost his mother when Basil was around two years old.

Basil knew exactly how to gauge his every emotion and would literally check on him every few minutes to offer him comfort, for many months, and in fact for the rest of his life, his main purpose seemed to be to honour and cherish all of us but most especially of all Simon.

We also adopted a very poorly German Shepherd puppy called Billy when Basil was around two years old, who came from the RSPCA after his mother had died of starvation soon after he was born. Billy was very frail but grew into a big strong boy. He lacked Basil's intelligence, and Basil literally had to teach him everything. They were sweet friends for many years and enjoyed good health, until sadly Billy developed health problems at a relatively young age, not only with terrible hips, but also with his immune system, which ultimately made him blind whilst he was still quite young.

As the years went by Basil became Billy's guide dog. We have been very lucky to live on a farm away from the roads, so they could both be loose and free range every day. Billy became very reliant on Basil, following him wherever he went. Basil always felt it his duty to look after everyone, not least Billy.

As Basil became older, steadily his body began to show the signs of old age. His paws would appear heavier and he developed a waddle, and grey hairs crept in where they had once been black. He seemed to manage fine for a long time, but the ageing then accelerated. He became more needier of Simon's company and needed more reassurance that he was ok, this seemed to always be his first priority in life.

He would trot along to the workshop by the house, where Simon would be stone carving, and check in on him to see all was well. This had always happened maybe four or five times a day, but towards the end of his life it would be every twenty minutes or so. Simon would take Billy and Basil for walks still, but these became shorter and confined only to flat fields as both old boys would struggle climbing the hills they used to bound up.

One awful day when Simon was away, I was feeding the dogs in the evening. Basil suddenly collapsed and began to have a huge seizure. I hadn't experienced this before, but soon learnt it was old dog vestibular disorder. I kept him as calm and comfortable as I could. He seemed very unwell and we were scared he was dying. He was unable to balance enough even to stand, and walking was almost impossible. Miraculously however, within a couple of weeks, he had almost completely recovered. He was even running around again, only now he had a tilted angle to his head and neck. This also recovered over the following weeks and months, but sadly later that year, the seizures returned. At first it was just one perhaps every few weeks, but in the very end they were happening several times a day. We knew he didn't have long left with us. It was terribly sad. He had been a part of our lives for sixteen years, and the children had never known life without him. We took every opportunity possible to make him feel loved and to know how much he meant to us all.

The day before he died, he became very weak. He lay on the grass in the sunshine, and we lay a light blanket over him.

The children lay on the ground beside him, just being there with him, and stroking his head. Simon too of course, spent some very precious minutes cuddling him and having a private cry together.

The following day, whilst the children were busy having their breakfast and rushing to get ready for school, Basil had made his way to Simon's workshop area. Simon was with him, and he called me on my mobile to quietly bring the children. The seizures were now relentless, and he was slipping away. It was the saddest thing taking the children out to gently and quietly kiss Basil goodbye. We each in turn kissed his forehead, told him through our tears that we would always love him, and then I had to leave Simon alone with him, as we were late for school by now. I drove away with tears streaming down my face, and felt terrible as the children got out of the car at school all in tears. They of course knew Basil was leaving us. Basil slipped away moments after we left. He died in Simon's arms being kissed and held closely. I know Basil never wanted to go, or felt that it was even acceptable. He felt such a duty and love for us all and of course for dear old Billy. It wasn't easy for him to let go, and we all had to let him know individually that it was ok for him to do this. I think the fact that it was just him and Simon at the very end, was what he would have wanted. Simon was in absolute pieces quite naturally.

We held a full family funeral for Basil that day after the children came home from school, each of us writing him letters and poems and covering his body in wild flowers from the field before he was buried. The whole place felt completely empty after Basil left, and that great void still remains.

Dear old Billy came into his own after losing Basil. We thought he would die the same week as he suddenly went very low, but he then found some kind of inner strength that he never knew he had. He made such an effort to join in with everything, despite his arthritis and blindness, and he even took on Basil's lifelong role of visiting Simon's workshop to check on him. We completely pampered him and gave him every treat we could, counting every day as an absolute blessing with him still with us.

Very sadly though, just five weeks later, Billy passed. He picked his spot outside, and lay down on the grass one summer afternoon. He waited until me and the children had all gone away to visit grandpa, and it was just him and Simon at home for a couple of days. Simon tried to bring him into the house, but he very strongly protested, so Simon carried a big mattress outside for him and helped him onto it. This was where Billy wanted to be. Simon put a big duvet over him and kissed him goodnight. That night Billy slipped away, warm under his duvet but under the stars above as he had chosen for himself. Perhaps it was easier for his spirit to take flight, being under the great canopy of the sky. He too had a full family funeral, and was buried next to his beloved Basil. He was fourteen.

An amazing and beautiful thing happened one week after Billy was buried next to Basil. Seemingly from nowhere, a wild red rose appeared growing from Basil's grave. The area had previously been thick with ivy and Simon had made the clearing for their burial sites especially. We had no rose bushes in the garden and certainly hadn't planted any. It seemed and felt like a parting gift from dear Basil. A symbol of his love.

He was a very special soul, so full of love for everyone always. He felt it was his job to make sure each and every one of us was ok on a daily basis, and to take away our sadness through difficult times.

We shall love him forever and miss him always. ♥

Gypsy
By
Collette Fergus

Gypsy first came into my life when I had just turned forty. I had just bought my own home, so finally could have a dog of my own. I looked around and found a litter of pups advertised close by. When I turned up at the house, there were three pure black German Shepherds in the litter. I had never seen a black one before, but immediately fell in love. She was such a large bundle of fluff. Her birthday was exactly the day before mine, so I felt it was meant to be!! She was so intelligent, and so quick to learn anything I taught her. She was every ounce amazing

Gypsy gave me unconditional love, and was always there for me when going through sad and traumatic times in my life. One time we went on holiday in Cornwall, I drove to the sand dunes and took her for a walk.

At one point during the walk, she disappeared and I couldn't find her anywhere. Eventually I had to walk back to the car, and report her lost. Low and behold, when I got back to the car, she was sitting there waiting for me!! We had never been there ever before, yet she had found her way back to my car?? She was an amazing dog. I also taught her the trick where when you went bang, she would fall down, roll over, and play dead. I could go for years without doing this trick, yet whenever I did it, she would always remember it, and play dead! She was also my very first dog, as I now I have a pack of dogs, but she will always have a very special place in my heart as was the first.

One of my traumatic times was when I lost my dogs for a year after they were stolen. I was devastated at the loss, but still had Gypsy to keep me strong. She gave me the strength to never give up the belief I would get my dogs back. And of course, I did get them back after a year, thanks to the help Gypsy gave me. She was a very special animal.

Gypsy went downhill within a week, it was so quick. It started off on a Monday. I went out for a walk and when I let her off, she didn't run off like she normally did. I thought that strange at the time. But then never thought any more about it, but then, during the week, she started to act more and more strangely.

She kept lying down, and not coming in from the garden. She was struggling to get up and walk by this time. By the Friday I was really worried, and took her to the vets. I always remember that Friday as it was my mother's birthday, and I was supposed to be going through to go out to lunch with her to celebrate her Birthday. My mum, was also severely ill at the time, had been diagnosed with pancreatic cancer.

I was still hoping that it would be something simple with Gypsy, and I would still get through to meet my mum. They said they would have to take her in and do some tests, so in the end had to hang around for hours to find out what was wrong. Then, unfortunately they gave me the tragic news, I just couldn't take it in, I was in total shock! They said that she had an enormous tumor that had ruptured and was bleeding internally. As it was in between her liver and spleen, they said there was nothing they could do for her, and said she must be put to sleep immediately. I couldn't accept it immediately, and to get it right in my own head, I had to be sure there was no other cure. So I asked if I could take her home to say goodbye. They gave me pain killers for her and she was booked in for the next morning.

The next morning arrived, which was now Saturday, but I was still not ready to let her go, I just couldn't face it, not today, I needed her a little longer, so asked if could bring her back on the Monday. Luckily, they agreed, and gave me more painkillers. I just couldn't accept it, the very thought of losing her was just too much. Sunday came, and by this time, Gypsy was really going downhill rapidly. I knew there was no hope, it wasn't fair to keep her like this and so it was time to let her go. It may sound horrible, but I was hoping the next morning would come quicker, as I couldn't bear to see her suffer anymore. In my deepest of thoughts I was hoping she would pass away at home where she was loved, rather than take that awful journey to the vets.

I kept visualizing her passing at home, it was what I felt was for the best, she was safe here.

She didn't disappoint me, it was as if she heard my thoughts, in fact I'm sure she did, as she managed to drag herself to my chair so she could be close to me.

Gypsy passed away peacefully on the Sunday night at home, loved and supported. I am sure she did this as she loved me so much. RIP Gypsy. The Pet Cremation took her away, and I got her ashes back in a lovely urn in the shape of German Shepherd, so she will always be with me. Obviously, I was devastated at losing her, she had left a large gaping hole in my life. I couldn't stop crying when she first got diagnosed and then when she passed, well, it was so very sad, but also I felt relieved in a strange way, as she was no longer suffering, and was finally at peace. So it was a strange bittersweet emotion.

2015 was a terrible year for me, as I not only lost my beloved Gypsy, but I ended up sadly losing my mum a few months later.

I have other dogs, but they all have their own special place in my heart.

Gypsy was one of a kind. Gypsy was always the one who came and laid her head on my lap when she knew I was upset. She was a very strong character, and could be a bit of a bully to the other dogs, but she was really a big softie, and had a heart of gold, and if a dog stood up to her, she would back down, and run off.

I guess my advice would be if you have already gone through a loss or are yet to face one is, never feel guilty that you had to make that awful decision, as you know it was the most loving thing you could do for your pet, even if you can't see it right now.

If I could say one last word to my Gypsy it would be this; I wish you were still here, but hope you are happy over Rainbow Bridge.

I love you, miss you, and will never forget you ♥

Pippa

By

Cheryl Murphy

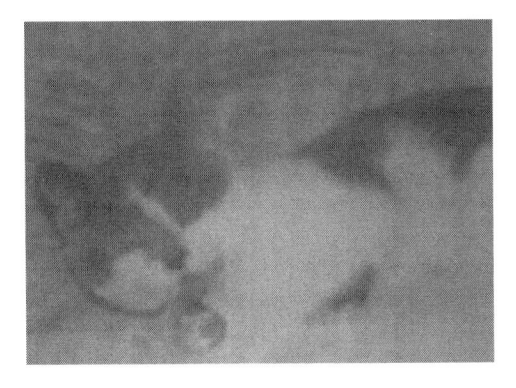

I saw an advertisement in a pet shop in Coventry for a grey and white kitten. And arranged to go and see her full of excitement. When we arrived at the house, Pippa was up a tree in the lady's garden and looked so cute. The lady told us that she had a couple who had already booked her for themselves, but at the last minute had changed their minds and so she now needed a loving home, so I believe it was fate and she was meant to come home with me that day.

We were so lucky to have her and fell totally in love with her straight away. And I will never forget the journey home that day either, as there were fireworks going off all over the sky, it was as if the universe was celebrating our new arrival and saying something like 'Welcome to your new family Pippa!'! She was so adorable.

However, whilst I like to think the fireworks were exclusively for us, it was more likely just to be because Bonfire night was just around the corner ☺ Pippa always recognized the sound of my car and even my parent's car when they came to visit, she loved them.

She would come running up to the car and climb in when we opened the door. I swear we could have lost her many times if we hadn't noticed she had jumped in! Pippa never, ever, stopped purring, seriously, it was all the time. She was so small for a cat, just the size of a kitten even as an adult and so very cute. Her beauty never ceased to amaze me; she truly was a beautiful cat, so pretty with lightening flash of white fur on her forehead just between her eyes.

Unfortunately, as she aged she eventually became ill; I was told by the vets that she had a serious kidney problem and that she really wasn't going to recover. I just didn't want to believe I was going to lose her, so I didn't. But one day after she had been diagnosed, I picked her up to put her into her pet carrier and made sure she was comfortable and cozy. Then, I drove to my parent's house to visit them taking Pippa with me, she loved being and the car and seeing my parents. When I got there, I picked her up out of her carrier and into my arms; but to my utter surprise; I could see she had already passed away! I just couldn't believe it. However, I do believe she waited so that I wasn't alone and I had my parents with me for support, I'm sure it happened that way, because I loved her so much. Obviously, I was absolutely devastated and heartbroken. She was my world, we had been through a lot together and she always seemed to know everything I said to her and helped me through some very tough times in my life.

Pippa was nineteen and a half years young, nearly twenty years old when she eventually passed. Some of my happiest memories were just cuddling her on my bed and all worries would disappear in the moment while she happily purred away from all the attention.

If I could give you anything, it would be to always keep your passed pet in your mind; you just never know when they may have to go. I miss you so much my Pippa angel and you will never be forgotten.

I love you tremendously, with all of my Heart.♥

Stella

By

Marina Brown

I had been waiting to get a bitch as I had a rescue boy who was then six years old; he was my first dog and felt that it would be nice for him to have a companion. My son introduced me to his friend, his family were expecting the arrival of puppies and it was the breed I had researched and felt it would be the perfect fit for my lifestyle

   I met Stella her at just two weeks old, I felt a connection immediately and just couldn't wait for the day when we would bring her home. Stella settled in very well, she and my dog became very close indeed, they were inseparable and as we proceeded with the training, it became more and more obvious she was very intelligent, loving and I felt she was almost human. She always seemed to know exactly what I was feeling. Stella was so obedient and I could walk her without a leash, it was like we were corded.

She adored all humans and one of the things I loved about her was when she would smile, her whole-body language was just amazing. Another thing I loved about her was she loved children, my grandchildren just loved her, she would sit with them on the grass over the park and would not leave their sides until they got up to walk on, then she would follow them. She also loved my horse; she used to drop her ball at my horse's feed bin whilst he was eating, like she was asking him to play ball with her. Stella taught me how to love, I'd had a bad childhood and had ended up with the biggest chip on my shoulder, but she changed that and brought out the love in me which I will be eternally grateful. We had cared for Stella from the age of six weeks, but when she reached eleven years old we noticed that her skull was sinking, it was just above her left eye. And after a few months of noticing it getting worse, I took her to the vet who then sent her to the specialist for an MRI scan, where it was sadly diagnosed that she had a brain tumour in the cranial part of her brain. They prescribed chemo, but I couldn't put this poison in her, I just couldn't! So, I found a lovely lady to do some holistic healing. The hospital had only given her about twelve months to live. I was naturally devastated of course, but I didn't think about it and just wanted to get her through the next twelve months as comfortable as possible. Stella went on to live for a further twenty-seven months; she was struggling with breathing which the vet said was lung disease, secondary to the brain tumour. Stella was struggling with her breathing now, she had arthritis and she looked so tired. I knew time was drawing near as when I looked into her eyes I could see it was time to release her spirit from the grip of the tumour.

I had contacted the Pet Cremation, advised them that I wanted an attended cremation for Stella, I couldn't bear the thought of taking her to the vet and then leaving her there for collection day. I had arranged for my vet to come to the house instead, so she would be surrounded by my other dogs and the grandchildren came the night before to say goodbye to her too which was sweet.

That morning, I think I just went into auto pilot, I laid on my bed with her, we hugged and I cried and we hugged some more until the vet arrived, she lay in my arms and the vet gave her the injection and I just cradled her, but felt she was free, free from that tumour, I cried and just said "run free girlie" run free. Then the next hardest part the attended cremation, it was so very dignified, she was placed in the chamber and the guy was so thoughtful and gentle, he blessed her and said go to the light Stella, we then had to go for two hours whilst they completed the cremation when they would then give us her ashes. When we returned home from the cremation, the house felt so empty, I felt empty, her energy had gone, it was awful, it really was. I couldn't stop crying, I could see her in every corner of the house. I could also see her in the park when I took the other dogs out. Everywhere was empty. All I could think of was Stella, I thought we'd be together forever. She's always in my thoughts. All thirteen years were happy, so many memories, we used to take her swimming, she loved her ball, our kisses and cuddles.

Advice I'd give to others who have lost their pet, is to talk about them, talk as if they were there next to you, cry when you want to and don't hold back any tears, tears are so very cleansing and will allow you to heel.

I wish I could just hold you Stella and walk with you one more time. Our love will never die, ever. Can't wait to see and hold you again Stellabells!

I love you Stella now and forever ♥

Thunder

By

Paul Oakley

Thunder, Thunnybuns, Buns 26/03/1996 - 11/08/2014

Thunder first came to me when she was about three-four months old. It was a weekend and I was sitting in the back garden in the sun with some friends when my next-door neighbour looked in. He was with his cousin who had rescued a kitten – her neighbours had gone on holiday and left their kitten shut in a room with some food and water and a litter tray lined with newspaper. The cousin was asked to look after the house while they were away, but when she found the kitten decided that enough was enough, apparently the kids had also been known to throw the kitten against the fence and see if the dog could get her. The cousin brought the kitten with her to see if anyone would re-home her. Even at three months Thunder was tiny and could fit on my hand, she had attitude though, as she also managed to seriously scratch the hand of my neighbour's cousin!

Even though she was always a small cat, she never lost that attitude. As soon as I saw Thunder I said I would give her a home and when I heard how she'd been treated I knew I wanted to look after her. It was love at first sight.

For several years, before I met the wonderful woman who is now my beautiful wife, Thunder was my only companion. We looked after each other and kept each other company, and I always made a point of spending time playing with her as soon as I got home from work, in retrospect, perhaps too much time, as she never quite got to understand the difference between the toy she was attacking and my hands! From the moment she was big enough to jump on my bed (with the help of a carefully placed box...) she slept on it, usually starting off by putting her paws on my hand which was on the pillow, and then her head on her paws. Later, she would move to a chair at the foot of the bed, but in the morning she would be back to be right next to me again.

When she first came to me I kept her in the bedroom to begin with, but she liked to explore, and one of the funniest memories I have is waking up in the middle of the night to see the door swinging open with Thunder hanging onto the handle by one paw as she'd worked out how to open the door! She liked to explore the outdoors too, but she was also very much a lap cat and would sit with me watching TV. One of the main reasons that helped me stop smoking was seeing the layer of smoke in the room at the end of the evening while Thunder lay on my lap, and thinking, this isn't fair on her, she is breathing this in as well. She was with me through some harder times and through the best times.

When Thunder was eighteen, she still had plenty of fight and life left in her. We were giving her tablets for high blood pressure and these were working, in fact, she was remarkably healthy for her age! She started to get an abscess on her gum, but it didn't seem to be bothering her. We mentioned it to our vet, and were told that due to her age it wasn't a good idea to operate as they would need to give her a general anaesthetic. Eventually though, it started to affect her ability to eat and she was losing weight. We had tried to feed her with a syringe, but it was almost impossible to give her enough food and it was causing her a lot of distress. The vet agreed to operate and all seemed well and Thunder even started to eat a little more and with homeopathic remedies and Reiki helping as well, she was beginning to put on a little weight.

A couple of days later though, the stitches came undone and she stopped eating again. We tried again to get her to eat but in only a few days she was fading away again. We had an appointment booked with the homeopathic vet, but when we took her there, the vet said there was nothing else that could be done, and now was the right time to say goodbye. I stayed with Thunder through to the end; she was eighteen and half years old.

The things I missed most were her not being in her basket under my desk at home, or lying on the back of the sofa, and not seeing her at weekend mornings, when she would still lie down with her paws in my hand on my pillow. I felt guilty in a way, because there was a certain amount of relief that it was over, and I felt angry and frustrated because if the stitches hadn't come undone she still had plenty of life left in her.

Over all that though, was sadness because of all the time we'd had together, but happiness that she'd had a happy home with me and a wonderful home after I met my wife Brenda.

It's difficult to pick a single memory as our time together was one long happy memory, but the way she used to 'bob' across the garden to come to the back door always made me smile, a sort of an eager bouncy trot that seemed to say she was really happy to see you.

My advice to you is; don't feel guilty for making the decision to say goodbye. There is never a right time and you'll always question whether it was too early or too late. Don't be ashamed to cry and don't let anyone tell you your animal wasn't important. And if I could say one last thing to my beautiful Thunder, I would just say; "Thank you"

I love you Thunder ♥

Gina

By

Ashley Frescura

Gina was my Christmas gift. She was given to me by my then sister in law who was a cook at a local restaurant. Funnily enough, the restaurants days' 'SPECIAL' just happened to be "whistle dogs!" a Canadian hot dog with odd toppings. When I walked into the restaurant that night, I could hear a puppy howling. It was ironic and funny to say the least. And out from the back came this little fur ball puppy with a green collar and a red bow. She curled up under my neck and kissed my face nonstop, like she knew I was her mom. She was and will always be my best Christmas gift, EVER!

From the time she was a puppy, Gina would curl up in bed with me. I can't even count how many times I woke up with her neck across mine sleeping so peacefully. Even when she was going through her energetic puppy stages, yes, you all know what that is like, she just seemed to know whenever I had a horrible migraine or feeling ill, she would settle down and just curl up on the couch comforting me till I felt better. She just seemed to know.

Gina got sick one Christmas Eve. After talking her to the vet she was put on a white rice diet with chicken breast.

By Christmas night she seemed to be doing better, so I assumed she had a stomach bug.

When we woke up on December 27th I soon realized it wasn't just a stomach bug. Because now, she was throwing up blood. I rushed her to the emergency vet, and after tests and a day of us cuddling on the exam room floor together, the vet very sadly informed me that Gina was very sick and the humane thing to do would be to put her to sleep. Laying on the floor by her side, I kissed her and told her I loved her, I told her that she was a very good dog and how sorry I was that this was happening. I held her head in my hands and told her how lucky I was to have her, I couldn't have asked for a better best friend. I told her what a good girl she was and that I loved her over and over again until I saw the light in her eyes go.

After Gina passed I laid and cried into her big mane of fur. I kept telling her to wake up! that I couldn't go on without her, that I wasn't strong enough on my own. When I finally left, I stood outside the vet's office frozen. I just couldn't believe that I came into the office with my best friend and I was now leaving alone. I knew that Gina was gone, but it took every rational thought in my body to not run back inside and get her, bring her with me, so I could leave the office like we came in... Together! I was totally heartbroken.

I have some wonderful memories of her, for instance, when Gina was just a few months old, I came home one night to a very hyper puppy. She was running laps around my living room up on the couch jumping across and landing on my coffee table before doing another lap and starting all over again. When I finally got a hold of this little 20 lb ball of energy I realized her face and paws were full of white sugar that had crystallized. Looking around the room I realized there was sugar everywhere!!!!

She had got up on the counter and tore apart a bag of sugar all over the first floor of my house and I mean all over!

After contacting the vet for advice and reassurance, we knew luckily she would be ok; I put her on her leash and tied her up in the kitchen to keep her out of the way of the clean up.

After a good two hours of cleaning up sugar I was exhausted and flopped down on the sofa just in time to see Gina walk into the living room dragging a half-chewed dog leash behind her. She stopped at the bottom of the stairs turned and looked me in the eyes. To this day, I swear she told me "I know I was bad but I'm going to bed" and up to bed she went. I still laugh every time I think about that puppy chewing through her leash so she could put herself to bed.

It's only been two days without Gina as I write this and the guilt I feel is horrible I wake up every hour questing if I did the right thing for her that last day. I can't say I have any advice for others right now, but I hope it gets easier for you. The only thing I can say for sure is I'm so great full that I took photos our last day together, photos of her, photos of me and her and a photo of when she put her paw in my hand. The photo of her paw and my hand is my greatest comfort right now. I look at that picture and know she wasn't alone at the end and that I loved her as much as she loved me. That photo is my most prized position now.

My message to my beautiful Gina, 'Even though People came and went from our life, you were always there for me, right by my side. I am eternally grateful to be able to call you my best friend. Thank you for all the joy you brought to my life. Gina, I am so sorry our life changed over the last few years, I am sorry I didn't know you were sick. You make me smile every day since the moment I walked into that restaurant. I love you so much! You were such a gentle soul, I will never forget you.

I love you♥

Rizzo

By

Sharon Lawrence

I first met Rizzo when I started to dog sit for him and his other doggie companion Paddy, a Red Setter. I've never seen such a beautiful dog in my life. Rizzo had this gentle energy around him; he wasn't scared but so unloved. We looked at each other, when our eyes met something happened, something I've never experienced before. That look went beyond all known communication, my heart started beating faster, my breathing changed, nothing existed around me, no noise, nothing. When I looked at him I could see something was happening to him also, it was like our souls had just blended, I saw a relief go through his body, we immediately had this knowing but when I went to touch him and he stepped back, his head lowered and he cowered.

I started to cry because this beautiful boy had never been touched, his owner always turned her nose up at him. She admitted she hated him and only liked her Red Setter Paddy and that Rizzo was just her boy friend's dog.

I loved Rizzo from the first time we looked at each other; it was like he became a part of my soul, my whole existence I looked after him twice a week, then I couldn't bear to hand him back knowing what he was returning to a kitchen with no toys and stuck in there for 12 hours a day. I asked if I could have them from Monday to Friday, they deliver Rizzo and Paddy on Monday morning and collected them Friday evening after work. Our bond deepened, it was like he could read my soul, and he could read my thoughts

One day I met a lady called Carol, she had two Italian Spinones, Rebus and Brando. My Rizzo went off sniffing and she got quite concerned that he went off doing his thing. "Don't worry" I said, I called his name and from at least 100 yards, he came bounding back bypassing and weaving past people and their dogs, nothing else mattered to him but getting back to me. He sat by my side, looking at me almost saying 'are you okay?'. Carol's face was in total shock, he only wanted me nothing else existed such was our beautiful bond. Carol and I became close friends after that and started walking together. Paddy always did his thing on walks, he was a good boy but Rizzo never liked to leave me, we just talked through our minds as I stroked him and my body just relaxed, I always got a lump in my throat because I loved him so much, so deeply, such was our bond.

One weekend I was told the owners were leaving the dogs to visit relatives; I couldn't bear the thought of Rizzo being left in that kitchen again. I decided I would have the dogs with me, I went to their house and sat in the kitchen, Rizzo and Paddy were in the garden.

As I sat there, Paddy came to the back door, he just stared at me, unable to move, then Rizzo came and did the same, it was like something out of cartoon. They froze on the spot looking at me. They've never seen me at their home before as they have always been dropped off at my home and couldn't comprehend what they were seeing.

We went outside and Rizzo just cried and cried, snuggling so deeply into me, Paddy wouldn't leave me alone either.

Their owners showed me something quite disturbing, Rizzo had dug a hole and put himself in it and refused to move from that hole, he was so depressed. They then asked if I would like to adopt them. I had no money, I couldn't afford the insurance let alone feed them but I was asked to think it over there wasn't any hurry. I went to everyone, even the RSPCA and everyone agreed if I couldn't financially support myself then how could I take on the insurance and care of two dogs, also I was a boxer dog person, my heart was with boxer dogs and I had rescued three in the past, I wanted another rescue boxer. So, I said I couldn't take them on, but had contacted Spinone Rescue via Carol, they said they had a home that was perfect for them both as they had to go together. Then reality sank in, I looked at Rizzo and I knew we were meant to be together as he knew what was going on, I could feel that in him, but I just couldn't, I had no money to support them. I then spoke with my mum, she couldn't understand why I was even thinking about it, she wanted me to just take them, but she did say "How could you let Rizzo go, he is so devoted to you and you to him".

The owners then said they would pay for both the dogs insurance for a year if I was to take them, I still couldn't afford them, but then I asked what Carol thought about the situation. I remember very well we were in her garden and she offered to pay for their food until I could afford it.

OMG, what a shocker, there was a possibility now, but what I wondered what would happen after the year? They would still need insuring after that and I couldn't keep accepting free food.

But also Rizzo didn't like cuddles and I needed a dog I could cuddle. As Rizzo was never touched, petting him was a strange experience and I needed to have a dog I could cuddle I went home so despondent, I had decided I couldn't have them, then I opened my emails and there was a "Thought of the Day" this email automatically sends you a daily message and that message that day made the decision for me.

It read; "money makes a good servant, but a bad master". I was allowing money to be my master, sent 19th August 2003, Rizzo and Paddy were mine in September 2003

Rizzo went on to become my Assistance Dog, he brought life back to me, and he always knew when I was going to have an episode and warned me. If I was angry he would calm me down, he made me focus on him. I have fibromyalgia and I'm very sensitive to being touched, he became that natural barrier to the world, nobody could bump into me anymore and cause such intense pain, going out became a frightening experience, but now he positioned himself between me and the people, keeping me safe. He did more than enhance my life, he gave me a life and together we went everywhere. I would say to him "Jacket" and he became so proud and excited to go out. When Rizzo finally allowed me to cuddle him, he bathed himself in cuddles. It was like he couldn't get enough and from then onwards we never stopped. But he never took to anyone else cuddling him, even my friend Carol who he loved, but would still not allow her to cuddle him. He took absolutely no notice of anyone who did stroke him, he didn't even acknowledge them.

He loved the back of my car too and I would leave the boot open for him to get in and out when he wanted. People loved it, he looked so cute, and he even let them stroke him, but didn't even bother to open his eyes to acknowledge them!

Luckily, I was the only person he had eyes for, nobody else existed Rizzo was a very spiritual dog who gave me so many memories, I can't pick one in particular but I loved it when he stepped onto my mobility scooter.

I praised him and from then onwards we would go on adventures sitting on my scooter footplate and he would rest his head lovingly on my legs. When we communicated, it was like a mind to mind conversation. When my mum's dog died, I said to him on the way to visit her, "Jake has died Rizzo and my mummy is very upset"
We pulled up got out of the car, went through the back gate and Rizzo ran in as normal but this time he went to find my mum, she was sitting in the kitchen. Rizzo ran to her rubbed his head on her leg and snuggled into her, WHAT! Rizzo never went to my mum, he would run in and go straight to the back room and go to sleep, he never, ever, interacted with her, I was the only person in his life. It was like he just knew what had happened.

The next time we visited he did just that, ran past and went into the back room and went to sleep! When Paddy was helped to cross over we were all together. When Paddy closed his eyes for the last time Rizzo was sitting with his head bowed so very low, he was sad. Then I said to him, "Say goodbye Rizzo." He looked at Paddy and very slowly he started lifting his head like he was following something, he lifted and lifted until he was looking at the ceiling. I had my friend Sharon Spence with me at the time, Sharon is a Spiritualist Medium and I said to her "did you see that?" she responded with "yes, I did." We were both amazed.

We woke up on Saturday 7th March 2015 it was just a normal day, nothing was the matter with Rizzo, nothing wrong with him at all, he was fit and healthy.

He had suffered from bloat the year before and was operated on, but recovered so well.

The strange thing about that was that I kept him rested for three days, just very short walks. Rizzo wasn't a social dog with other dogs, he only had eyes for me, he wasn't aggressive, and he just didn't care.

The day I took him to Horsell Common after his operation, he ran excitedly to every dog as if to say "I'm alive, I made it" I was so shocked I couldn't believe what I was seeing, Rizzo had no time for dogs or people, he did his own thing, yet here he was going to every dog so excited. He knew, I swear it, because on the next walk he didn't bother again, he was back to normal. After the bloating he did recover, then, I noticed he was becoming sluggish, he made a strange sound and I rushed him to the vets, it was on a Saturday, early evening. Gill his vet really examined him and said she wanted to scan him. It was then I heard her partner say "did you feel something?" and she responded "mmmmmm" Rizzo let her scan him, he was so good, but then Gill turned to me and said "I'm so sorry, but he has a tumour on his spleen and its 50/50 that he will live" I nearly died, no, this can't be happening! Not to my Rizzo. She wanted to operate but then she listened to his heart and it was irregular, he needed medication to stabilise it, but she said she didn't have any of the medication needed as she had run out on the Friday. She went away to see what alternative she did have and came back, the medication she wanted to bring she didn't have either and was very surprised and said "that's strange, I had to give another client another drug yesterday because we had run out." So, we couldn't operate on Rizzo. I went back on the Sunday and still Gill couldn't operate. A check up was arranged for the Monday, but I said I wanted him to have some healing before having the operation and so could I come later, so it was agreed I would take him for healing first, which I did.

We drove to the vets, the vet examined Rizzo and quite shocked she said the heart murmur has gone!

I can operate now because strangely I've had two cancelled operations this afternoon.

That was it I knew he was safe and everything was going to be fine and it was, Gill said "you're lucky it looks benign" and it was. Rizzo's health went from strength to strength after the removal of his spleen, he was a puppy again, and that tumour must have been making him so lethargic.

Anyway, several months later 7th March 2015 we had a lovely walk on the common.

Then went to the "Rock and Gen show" at Kempton Park, he sat with the event organisers Keith and Carole while I looked around, he got a bit restless and tried to find me, Keith came and found me and we left, he was so happy. I said to Rizzo "shall we have a Carvery?" and he looked as if he approved, so we drove there, he came in with me and within about forty five minutes, something happened to him, he couldn't walk, his back legs didn't work, so feeling worried, a few guests kindly helped me get him into the car and I drove straight to the vets without delay. The vet examined him and thought it was a nerve problem, he didn't think it was a stroke as his eyes were not flickering, so he gave me some medication and we went home. Rizzo struggled with his back legs, he couldn't walk so I got him up on the sofa in the lounge and let him sleep. Four hours later things went from bad to worse, he couldn't use his front legs now, so back and front had now gone. With help from my friend and neighbour, I drove him to the vets again. This time Pete the vet said it was indeed a doggie stroke and its possible he will recover in around 6 weeks, he will be totally incontinent an unable to move, he will lose all muscle tone if I didn't keep him exercised, I knew then I had to let him go.

I called my carer Ellis and she came straight away. Rizzo was so excited to see her, it was horrible to watch, she made him so happy and that was his last cuddle from her.

Pete sedated him and I cuddled him whispering sweet nothings in his ear, then the final injection and my world fell apart. The unthinkable happened, my invincible immortal Rizzo had died, and he was gone. How could my Rizzo be so healthy and happy in the morning and be dead in the evening? Not only had I lost my best friend, family, confident and assistance dog, my life, as I knew it went that day also. I couldn't leave my Rizzo there at the vets, we were never apart and it wasn't going to happen now. So, I took him home.

We laid Rizzo out in my conservatory, with angels and candles and I announced on Facebook that "Rizzo's Dead". The telephone never stopped ringing, messages poured in because he was a star on Facebook, everyone knew he was my assistance dog and shocked waves ran through my friends. Suddenly I was on my own, sitting in the bathroom, then I heard dog paws on the carpet trotting up and down, that distinctive noise I used to hear when we played fetch, it was like he was searching for me. I froze and didn't know what to say, I didn't want to make a noise to disturb him but then that was it, the footsteps stopped and I've never heard him again I took Rizzo to the crematorium and I was on my own, my carer couldn't come as she had another arrangement and no matter how much I begged her, keeping the arrangement with another friend was more important, I told her to go, I was angry, I didn't want her near me. I felt let down. I was on the M3 motorway talking to my friends on my hands free, crying and crying, why am I on my own? I was devastated. The telephone conversation kept me going, kept my mind on the road, but still I kept shouting "I'm on my own". Then, just after the motorway turnoff a song came on the radio "I will always love you" and I couldn't breathe, this was a song I had played at my husband's funeral eleven years ago. The song finished ten seconds after turning up at the crematorium, I knew then I wasn't on my own, Ted my husband was with me.

The feeling of loss was indescribable, emptiness, loss of a friend and confidant but also my assistance dog. My life when down to a level I didn't think people could get to. I went into a bubble and learnt how and why people committed suicide. You go into this bubble. The bubble was addictive, no noise, nothing but calm, nothing existed outside of this bubble. The strange and sheer silence of your mind and the pain and anger had gone. This bubble was so calm and peaceful and I didn't want that feeling to end. I eventually came out of the bubble because my carers touched me, they had called, but I didn't answer and the reality of life without Rizzo came back. I was so low and soon underwent psychiatric care, put two stone of weight on and hardly left the house. I didn't wash or dress for many days and my carers couldn't make me. But, because of Rizzo being my owner trained assistance dog, I wasn't going to let his death be in vein. I started my cause "**Rizzo's Legacy**" where I became an owner trained assistance dog warrior, fighting the discrimination against us. I stopped people from becoming evicted because council and housing assistance didn't know the law and thought ADUK charity were the authority on assistance dog's when they were not. Taxi drivers and shops all got letters from me then I started on the government. Working with my MP Jonathon Lord, he was amazing and supported my cause as did Dogs Today Magazine, we worked on the government. We were determined for the government to accept owner trained and not think because we never went through a charity we were any less qualified than ADUK accredited charity partnerships.

    I began to challenge the whole system, writing to ADUK, EHRC and EASS anyone who could give me advice and on 02.02.2017 I attended a meeting at Caxton House to hear that the new disabilities minister wanted to see the way forward with owner trained assistance dogs. We did it!

I've taken up a cause to get owner trained assistance dogs accepted and on 2.2.2017 I was in a meeting with DWP advisers about assistance dogs. My MP and I have been working so hard on this. Rizzo was an <u>owner</u> trained assistance dog and I was determined his life was going to mean something.

    I have so many memories, but I loved seeing Rizzo sunbathing in the boot of my car, I loved hearing him howl, but most important of all, the communication we had because I believed in and we were so open. Rizzo knew the difference between "I love you" he wouldn't make any movement when I said it, he just accepted love. If you said "do you love Mumma?" he would always jump up and give me so much love and be so excited. He knew the difference all right

    I can't find any advice to give if you are grieving yourself; we are all different and depending on how your beautiful pet died depends on the type of advice. But to help them crossover is the biggest selfless act you can give. Maybe go and help another unwanted animal, give them the home and love that your beloved pet was honoured and that they would approve of you saving the new animals life.

    I have a message for my Rizzo, "I know you're watching and helping me, but I can't feel you, please come closer so I can feel you, please? Please help me with Ottie, my new boy, he needs your guidance; teach him to be as a good assistance dog as you were. And ask Ottie to trust me more and together we will see the world, so he can experience all the privileges an assistance dog has. Tell him that noise is not going to hurt him, just look and trust in me like you did Rizzo. When my time comes please meet me, I love and miss you so much, I really do. Thank you for all your help with 'Rizzo's Legacy', we will make a change and your name Rizzo, will never be forgotten

I love you Rizzo ♥

Geronimo

By

Brenda Oakley-Carter

Geronimo (aka Ronnies, Geronimozie) 29/03/2008 - 13/06/2010

I volunteered at an animal rescue where I did dog walking and offered Reiki to all the animals. A feral cat had kittens and two were ginger boys who captured my heart from day one. They had very different personalities, Geronimo was all action and adventure, he fell out of the cage they were in and his brother Raffey was a little kitten of Zen, hiding behind all of them. Ronnies (Geronimo) was full of life, mischief, joy, energy, and adventure.

Everything was full on. He made us laugh so much as he had no awareness of his 'naughty' Behaviour, whether he was knocking all the cards off the mantelpiece or pouncing on everything that moved.

He liked to explore everything he even fell out of an upstairs, open bedroom window when he was a kitten which terrified the life out of me but he was absolutely fine. He gave himself a little shake, washed a paw and walked back into the house! He really was a 'Geronimo'!! He would sit on top of post of the banister at the top of the stairs and chase his tail...we all used to be so scared when he did it but he was always ok. He would also run along the garage roof without fear. He loved to go out, and later, sometimes for a night or two which would leave us frantically looking for him, but he always came back, exhausted.

Unfortunately, Geronimo was hit by a car, about half a mile from our house. It was 1pm on a Sunday afternoon when we got the awful phone call. We have no idea why he was so far away, apart from maybe he was visiting the farm that is along there. The driver of the car didn't stop but a lovely couple in the car behind did, checked his collar and rang us. It was like the world had stopped. We went to him immediately and saw his little ginger body, lying by the side of the road. I was praying that they were wrong and that we could still save him, but no. He did look peaceful and almost untouched. We sat and held him gently when we got home cuddling him and telling him we loved him. We were in such shock though. The immense shock and intense grief engulfed me and was almost too much too bear. I struggled to come to terms with it for a long time afterwards. How could this happen to our Ronnies? He was only two and full of the joys of life...how could he be gone?

That night our four remaining cats all came and slept on the bed together, they'd never done that before. It was so hard to see the mourning of his brother Raffey went through.

On the day after, he slept with our cat Herbie (who he never really went near) and buried his face in Herbies fluffy tail, almost hiding. He was depressed and looked for Ronnies for a long time after.

One day, months on, I was watching an old video of Raffey and Ronnies playing and Geronimo's collar bells were jangling...Raffey came running into the room when he heard that and ran straight up to the TV where the sound was coming from. He still knew those were Ronnies bells. That was heartbreaking to see. I found help from the Cat Chat website on their Rainbow Bridge page where other people who had just lost their cats also went...the support and love there made such a difference to me.

One memory I have is when we had just got a new mattress and the old one was temporarily on the landing until we could get the council to take it away. It became one of Geronimo's favourite places to sit. Every time one of us walked by and he was there, if we hadn't noticed him and didn't fuss him, he'd run along the length of the mattress beside us and stick a little paw out, with claws, to catch our clothes to make us stop so we'd fuss him. He was so funny, so cheeky. He was such a character and we loved him so very much.

If I was to give you some advice, just do what you need to do to get through. Find websites with Rainbow Bridge pages and get support from other animal lovers who have been through it or are going through the same. Go through old photos, videos etc Cry. Cry. Cry. It can't be rushed. My husband made a lovely video from clips of our cats set to music. It's called Cattitude, by Paul Oakley and is very joyful, with happy memories. You can find it by typing this address into your address bar of your internet browser;

HTTPS://www.youtube.com/watch?v=qfj1sbYVA90

My message to Geronimo is that we love and miss you, but hope you are happy, safe and loved. Thank you for coming to see me in my dreams sometimes. I will always remember you.

I love you♥

Horatio

By

Brenda Oakley-Carter

Horatio, aka Mr Raich, Horatio Toe! 8/4/1993 - 27/1/2011

My vet mentioned that his cat had had two kittens that they were keeping, but it might be nice for me to have one and he said he'd bring this little one round, just so I could meet him. Well, it was love at first sight. Horatio was funny, very gentle and had the most beautiful energy about him.

Horatio was the gentlest, most peaceful and calm cat that I've ever met but had his 'mad' moments too, which seemed extra mad as he was usually so chilled out! He just went about his business with no fuss, no drama, just calm. He always slept with my young son, on his pillow every night, right up to the year before he died and then he would come in with us on the pillows where we would be lucky to get an eighth of the pillow with Raich sprawled out over the rest! He never caught any wildlife and even if he tried to 'stalk' a bird, his vertical, on the spot sudden leaps would scare the birds before he ran at them.

In fact, he was such a 'no threat' that the birds didn't even fly off when he was out in the garden.

All our cats (we had four others) were happy to sleep with him and seemed to seek him out. They didn't sleep with each other though.

Horatio started to get kidney trouble when he was thirteen, but we were managing to keep it controlled but four years later other things started too. He had arthritis which was difficult to help, as he couldn't take Metacam because of his kidney problem. We managed the symptoms and pain with acupuncture and Reiki which really helped for a time. He then had a couple of fits and we knew there wasn't long left. His appetite was going and we fed him a warmed, liquid food and squirty cream which he loved. His dirt tray was right by his bed and we had constant heat pads and waterproof sheets under his blankets so he was as comfortable as possible. He just wasn't really 'with us' on the last couple of days, only having a little squirty cream off our fingers, we really hoped he would pass naturally but it wasn't fair to him when he didn't, so we called the vet. As we waited for the vet to come we played beautiful, quiet, soothing music and lit lots of candles. Although so very sad after eighteen years, we were relieved that he wasn't suffering or struggling any more. His peaceful little presence was hard to be without and our other cats notice his absence too. He had always been 'everywhere' in our home.

Horatio is our huge happy memory, everything he was. The dearest, funniest being, who once gently but determinedly forced his way onto my lap as I was giving Reiki to our sick hen, he didn't mind who was there and happily snuggled beside her, he just wanted a lap!

Enjoy every moment when your animal is alive. Make them as comfortable as possible as they come to the end of their days with you and know the bond live on.

Time really does help but the love never dies. I'd like to say this to my boy, "I hope you're safe and well and very loved wherever you are.
We love you so much and will never forget you".

We love you ♥

Zoe

By

Kay Stack

My beloved Zoe was born on 3rd of Feb 2000. She was a free to good home puppy, but came from a very loving and caring family. She was one of, I think, six puppies. Her mum's name was Charlie. Zoe was a black Labrador Retriever with a touch of sheepdog, which she inherited from her runaway daddy. She came to live with us as a six weeks old puppy on the 16th of March. She reminded me of my very first stray doggy Fuga, which I also asked to teach Zoe everything... She was my girl...she was my friend...she shared her life with her cat brother, Mulder, who will turn 18 on April 22, 2017.

My precious Zoe gave me so much love and joy...I have tears in my eyes writing this...I look at her photo everyday...I miss her so very much...She always followed me everywhere I went, she was my little disciple...she didn't like the "Happy Birthday Mr President" song by Marilyn Monroe, she'd go barking like mad if we started to sing it!

Unfortunately, Zoe got unwell and we did all we could to save her...she had leukaemia and died on the 10 August 2009 at 1 pm in my arms on the sofa in the living room.

I didn't want her to suffer anymore and I asked the Angels to take her...and they did...I didn't go to work that day, I begged my manager for an extra day off as I had been on holidays the previous week, as if I knew this was going to be the last day with my beautiful girl, my life turned upside down as that year was one of the worst too. I also had a car accident, but the Angels saved me and later my ginger cat Dancer went over the Rainbow Bridge too. Zoe was buried in my friend's garden together with her own pets. I lost my little girl and Mulder lost his doggy sister, he grew up with. I just want to hug her again so much, I miss her so much, I asked her to please find me someone to love. And she found me ASH Animal Rescue in Co. Wicklow and lots of doggies and other pets to love, she found me my rescue doggies, Sasha and Aaron.

"I will never forget you Zoe. Mummy loves you very much Please watch over your little siblings". I write this with a very broken heart and tears.

I love you Zoe ♥

TeddyBear Snarfles

By

Jennifer Stephens

I decided to foster TeddyBear Snarfles when he was saved a few hours before being euthanized. When he first came to me I didn't think I would ever be able to touch him. He had been labelled with an aggressive problem, but he wasn't aggressive at all. Being a double coated Pomeranian, TeddyBear Snarfles was one big mat, and so it was so important that I had him shaved down and groomed. He certainly was a lot happier. I was only to be a foster but two days later my daughter was saying "Mom, TeddyBear Snarfles can't go with someone else, they won't love him like we do" So a foster fail I became. I fell in love with TeddyBear Snarfles in his photos but he took my heart when I finally saw him.

TeddyBear Snarfles had the biggest impact on my life, I knew from the beginning after his first vet appointment that whatever time we had, I made a promise to him he would always be loved and he would never suffer. He took over me by his little snarl dance he did when you came home from somewhere, it was so cute! I had always known since the first vet appointment that he had disc degenerative disease. I knew from the beginning there wasn't a cure either. There was no surgery that would help and no amount of time that would change what ultimately would take him from me. At first it was four or five bones fused together but by June 1st 2016 at the vet appointment, it had turned into six or seven bones fused together and hairline fractures in his spine. Our vet told us he only had about six months to a year left to live and there was a decision we would have to make, the vet told us that she was there for us when the time came. When the pain killers stopped working and the fear he would break his back by jumping the wrong way started, my head took over because my heart couldn't make that decision. And so, on July 11th 2016 at 4:10 P.M. TeddyBear Snarfles left my life and took my heart with him. My life crumbled, basically I died inside. Waking up the next morning and not seeing his snarl dance killed me. My memory of him was two and a half years of every moment with TeddyBear Snarfles. I didn't have one, I had a million. If I could tell anyone anything, I'd just say keep your promises to them, even if you have to make the decision to let them go with love and dignity. Tell them how much they are loved and tell them how proud you are of them for rescuing you. Yes, they come into our lives when we need rescued and always remember they only truly go home when their wings are ready. My message to my boy is "TeddyBear Snarfles mama loves you, I know you have been leaving signs; I hope you're happy and pain free now and I pray when I let you go you truly knew that I did it out of love."
I will always love you ♥

Tiddles

By

Sandra Kay

Tiddles arrived in my life on a motorbike, when I was about four or five years old. She had been living as a stray in the tyre-fitting garage where my mum worked, but it wasn't a very safe place for a cat with all the cars and trucks driving in and out all day. Our cat had died a few months earlier and my mum decided we should offer this stray a home. She arranged for one of the men at the garage to bring her to our house, so Tiddles was bundled safely in a box and put in the motorcycle sidecar for the journey. I don't remember much about our earliest days together or who named her as I was very young at the time, but I do know that we soon formed a strong bond which lasted for the rest of her life. Tiddles was my constant companion throughout my childhood and teenage years. I grew up with her. I was an only child and I called her 'my sister'. She was always sitting on my lap. We played together. Her favourite game was chasing a piece of string that I pulled underneath the door. She slept on my bed and put up with everything I did to her, including wheeling her around in my doll's pram. She was a terrific hunter.

There was a big area of rough ground behind our house and some pens where people kept chickens, pigeons and a goat so there were plenty of mice for her to catch. She would bring them home to our garden to try to teach me how to catch them. I remember the time we came home to find Tiddles proudly showing off to us the row of three headless rats she had carefully lined up on the back doorstep. She was strong and fearless. Dogs used to give her a wide berth. If they got too close, she would go for them, regardless of their size, and more than one dog ended up running off with a scratched nose. Tiddles taught me about life. Times were different then and for many years the vet refused to sterilise her. When she started calling we tried to keep her in, but sometimes she would escape and then inevitably there would be another litter of kittens. I watched them being born. We made her a nice comfy bed in the kitchen, but she would always carry the newborn kittens one by one upstairs and settle down with them under my bed. She wouldn't let anyone near them except me.

By the time I went away to university, Tiddles was a very old cat. I didn't want to leave her and I missed her terribly. Each time I came home I just wanted to be with her again and I know she was thrilled to have me home. Each time I could see how much thinner and older she had become, but I didn't realise I was losing her. It was early in the summer holidays after my first year away that she passed. Tiddles was curled up in her box in the kitchen when I went to bed that night. I woke up in the early hours and heard her calling for me in my mind, but I was very tired so I said "Go back to sleep sweetheart, I'll see you in the morning". But next morning my dad came to tell me that he'd found her dead in her box. She had passed in the night. I think she waited for me to be home before she died. I was devastated. I have always regretted that I didn't get up and go down to her that night. I'm sure she called out to me to say goodbye as she died.

I wished I could have been with her during that final year. I hated leaving her behind. The main reason I came home during term time was to see Tiddles and after she died I didn't come home as often. I always wondered whether she understood why I wasn't there anymore.

My main memory of Tiddles is just her always being there as I grew up and playing our favourite games together.

I would advise anyone who has lost a pet to arrange for an **Animal Communicator** like **Joanne Hull** to contact them. It is such a great comfort to hear from them again. I've done this for my pets who have passed in recent years, but I've only just found out that I could also do this with Tiddles, who died so long ago. I always thought too many years had passed, but I look forward to being able to speak to her soon.

The one thing I would say to Tiddles, is that I'm so very sorry for not coming downstairs to her on the night she died and thank her for saying goodbye to me.

I will always remember you and love you ♥

Cassie

By

Steve & Fiona Minion

Cassie came to us via a friend whose dogs had a litter. She initially went to our friend's brother, but they had just had a baby and felt they wouldn't be able to cope, much to our delight and benefit. We'd never had a rottie before although they were a firm favourite breed of ours.

From day one she bonded with our old boy Billy and enriched our life every day of hers. She loved the beach on holidays and romping in the snow in winters. Our abiding memory was her 'breaking' dad. He had vowed never to feed a dog from the table and he never did..... until Cassie came along! Cassie was sadly diagnosed with pancreatitis and for a while she was OK.

She suddenly went downhill, we took her to the vets and they had her in for the afternoon for tests and X-ray's.

My husband and I were in the next town, he was having her tattooed on his arm when we got the call telling us that she was riddled with cancer.

We decided she was too precious to allow her to suffer so said kit goodbyes that same day. She was a week short of her eighth birthday. We were bereft losing Cassie. She was the love of our lives, although we had other dogs, she was a special, very special animal. She also dispelled stereotypes regarding Rottweiler's. She was gentle, loving without a nasty bone in her body.

We had so many happy memories with her; she particularly loved our holidays to the seaside and always expected to share my husband's ice cream cone.

One piece of advice I would give people who experience loss is to get another dog as soon as you can cope, but not the same breed as it wouldn't be fair to the dog you have now.

If I could say one thing to Cassie, it would be that we love her so very much and were sorry we didn't have more time with her

We will always love you ♥

Fred

By

Margaret Khoja

I saw Fred one day in the window of my local pet store which sold puppies. He seemed to be looking at me. I passed that store a few times yet every time I walked past there he was, just looking at me. Eventually, I went in and asked his price, I wasn't sure I could afford him so I went to the bank to see how much I had available. I was a little worried by buying this dog it may just leave me financially short! It turned out after checking my balance that I really couldn't afford him. So, I went back to the pet store heavy hearted, and nearly bought another cheaper dog. But all the time I kept looking at Fred I knew he was the one for me, I mean how could I not buy him, he was the whole reason I was in the pet store in the first place. So, I changed my mind and Fred and I were together at last. I also had three wonderful cats at that time, and when I brought Fred home, all of them took turns to box his ears. Not hard, I guess it was a little warning to say 'Oi you, we rule this house!' So Fred very quickly knew where his place was in the pecking order of the house. The cats ruled.

Fred was an amazingly good dog.

I used to watch Law and Order each night at 11pm. And as soon as he heard the music, he would trot out and sit with me on the couch. We would share a Twix bar.
(*Nobody had told me about dogs and chocolate, that it was actually poisonous for them! But thankfully he was ok*) Later one of the cats was injured and had to have the left front leg amputated. When the cat returned from the vet, she was all bandaged up and, of course, limping. Fred put his nose when the leg used to be, and helped her to walk. If I hadn't seen this with my own eyes, I wouldn't have believed it. They became close companions from then on.

A few days before we lost her, I dreamed her mother and siblings came to my front garden to look for her and she left with them. I never really thought much of it at the time, but a few days later something strange happened, my Fred lost use of his legs. I took him straight to the vet, who told us he unfortunately had a spinal virus that he couldn't cure. So, I and my son held him that day for the last time. We said goodbye to our much-loved boy. He was fourteen years old. We cried and cried for days.

Even to this day when I see a Cocker Spaniel, I remember my wonderful dog. I still miss him to this day.

I love you Fred ♥

Blaze

By

Pary Draper

Would you believe I found her on Facebook, she was a tiny puppy that had been rescued from a home that was no good to her, but luckily, she was days old when they found her and we didn't have to suffer trust issues or any other complications. I knew immediately when I saw her she would be my baby Blaze. Blaze changed my life drastically when I got her, it was like she knew that I needed her. And let's face it, who doesn't love puppies?! With the puppy breath, those sloppy kisses and that fireball attitude she was a go getter. She was a wild one, but she would calm down for me and just knew when I needed some extra attention.

Unlike most in this book, I am pleased to say Blaze is still alive, but the day I found out I was going to lose her was the worst day I've experienced so far in my life. I made the most unselfish decision I could, I owner surrendered her, simply because I couldn't give her what she needed anymore. I had a change in life and had to move to an apartment and for a Rhodesian Ridgeback mix that just wasn't going to work.

My heart felt like it was ripped out of my chest, like I was losing my own personal shrink, (she knew everything)
I cried myself to sleep when I decided it was time for her to meet new people and have a life of "non-apartment living" I can't even begin to explain the pain. I came home that lonely morning and let me tell you, lonely doesn't even begin to explain my feelings. I quickly felt the emptiness. She wasn't there to jump on the couch wanting me to cuddle her. She wasn't going to wake me in the middle of the night barking at the TV. I won't get to hear those bells I have hung on the door for her to go potty. I just won't get to see her anymore. Even though she went to a great home, she wasn't my best friend anymore. And that was extremely hard to come to terms with.

If I had to think of one of the happiest moments we have had my mind immediately go to the time I was rearranging my bedroom and moved my bed, I had never seen so many toys, bones, socks, and so much more. The look on her face was priceless when she saw all the hidden treasures she herself had forgotten she had hidden! Boy, she was so comical.

If I could tell her anything today, it would be that I still think of her and miss her dearly and still want her back, truly I do. It really does get me so emotional thinking of her. As selfish as it is, I want her back with me, but she's in such a better place for her right now and that is the most important thing. I would tell her that I loved her so much; I had to make a decision and a decision that was right for her, not me. And I never wanted to give her up.

This was so hard to talk about. I cried the whole time I typed this.

I love you Blaze, now and always ♥

Arnold

By

Simone Howard

Arnold was fifteen. I had him for twelve years. He was a very special boy! I cried writing it, he was my best friend. No matter what was going on in my life he made me smile on my darkest days, there were a few! He was very popular with everyone, kind loving and always looking at you with a smile and his one eye (he had eye cancer and had to have it removed) The day he got it removed, when I picked him up from the vet, he went absolutely nuts when he saw me from sheer excitement! Even when he was not feeling well he would make sure he got up for cuddles

However, one day someone gave him a cooked bone and he ended up in the vet one very sick boy. ☹ He had to have a huge operation and died twice during this, but he did make it through the night. The next morning, the vet told me to come and see him but told me he would not know I was there, as he had a hard night and they had to keep him sedated.

Arnold did know I was there and tried to stand up, the vet was amazed! I kissed him, gave him hugs until I had to leave which was so painful.

As soon as I left him, he sadly passed away. The vet said he waited for me to say goodbye.

It's been four years now and I miss him every day. I find talking about him and seeing this picture reminds me of happy times I got to spend with my boy. He was and will forever be in my heart I have his ashes in my room under a framed picture, I miss him every day!

I will always love you Arnold ♥

ZARA: I met my beloved girl Zara through a friend which she belonged to and he had rescued her! I remember her huge personality and incredible intelligence. So much wisdom! As soon as we met it was a mutual respect with a bond and love being formed that would develop into a deep love and incredible devotion!

I will always remember her pregnancy and how huge she was and how difficult it was for her to move by the end of it. I spent ages rubbing her tummy gently and helping her get around. After that day, our bond became unbreakable and I knew from the look in her eyes the complete gratitude and respect that she blessed me with. From that day forth our bond became inseparable!

Zara taught me the true meaning of unconditional love too! What it means to be bonded and family! She was my special girl that understood me just from the look in my eyes! All I had to do was look at her and she knew exactly what I meant! Her intelligence was unmatched and her leadership skills were incredible! I never had to repeat a command.

She was my baby girl, best friend, fearless protector and companion! The most obedient girl I have ever met! She showed me what loyalty is! She was the easiest girl I could have wished for! Never a bother in the world! At bed time, she would get up, come over and give me a kiss and go to the bedroom! There will never be another incredible girl as my precious Zara that I loved dearly! Zara's loss was very unexpected and sudden! She was suffering from a disease that had gone undetected and was misdiagnosed! I had been running her around from doctor to doctor but all they could do was to give her pain killers.

One day her pain had become unbearable and I rushed her to hospital! They asked me to leave and that they will be in contact soon! I returned home and anxiously awaited the phone call to tell me the diagnosis!
I fell from the sky and was in total disbelief when I heard the words that she had suffered a heart attack and had passed away! I was in total shock and I didn't know how to process the information which seemed like I was in a surreal time warp listening to someone else's experience! I felt like fainting but I also became concerned about how Dino would accept her loss as he totally adored her! I decided that we should visit her together so he would understand why she isn't coming home. I didn't have time to properly grieve her loss because soon after, Dino became sick and I had to take care of him! It was brought on by the stress of losing his love, Zara! I felt like my heart had been ripped up, chewed up and spat out but I had to be strong for Dino! I would take him outside so I could cry in private but he knew as he too felt the pain of her loss and grief! Suddenly there was a massive void in our home and Zara's absence was hugely evident and deeply felt! She left a whole in my love that could never be filled!

My family was incomplete! My happiest and most cherished memories of my precious girl Zara are at the beach! She just loved to swim!

During our winter walks along the beach she would take off to go swimming and I would say "not today Zara, it's too cold" and she would return with a sad look on her face but was always obedient! During the summer though she loved it when I would throw large pebbles and she would actually dive into the sea and look underwater for it! If she couldn't find the same one she would bring me back another one! It makes my soul smile when I think of those cherished times together playing, swimming and running at the beach!

If I could tell my special girl Zara anything it would be simply be how much I love her! "Thank you my precious girl, for all that you were and for loving me unconditionally, as I loved you and for accepting me as I am! Thank you for being in my life! You were a true blessing and an absolute pleasure to know! I miss you more than words can express and not a single day passes that I don't think of you!
I hope you and Dino are up there playing and still by my side!"

I love you Zara ♥

Tom

By

Debbie Morcom

Tom Tom or Tommy Pom Pom, as we fondly nick named him. This pure black (well apart from a single white whisker) entered our lives on 1st December 2006. He had been Rehomed from the Cats Protection after his elderly owner passed away and the daughter could not look after him as she had young children. Tom had spent a fair amount of time at the Cats Protection on two occasions. We spotted Tom and fell in love with him immediately. One of the carers at the shelter could not believe we had managed to pick him up as he normally disliked anyone coming near, the rest is history. Tom was extraordinarily verbal, a real chatterbox.

He loved cuddles most of all and would poke/tap you with his paw until you picked him up for cuddles. He would settle within seconds and happily stay there for as long as you allowed him to.

Tom liked to lovingly nibble with his gummy drool (he only had one fang).

He had a real zest for life and made such a difference to our home. He was always about and his presence would fill a room. Tommy Pom Pom literally passed away in front of my eyes.

It was a Thursday evening when I was sat at my kitchen table with him, cuddled up beside me on the bench. He was nuzzling and asking for cuddles. I happily obliged and then gave him a brush. What happened next was truly heartbreaking. He jumped down, turned around and looked at me. In that instant, he literally dropped to the floor on his side. I dropped to my knees and went to pick him up, how he felt when I tried to pick him up is not one I had ever experienced. It was like picking up a scarf, this still haunts me. I tried to resuscitate him to no avail and quickly realized he was gone. I held him and then laid him down. I can remember looking at him and seeing that I hardly recognized him now, that his soul had left his earthly body behind.

Tom went to sleep on 21st March 2013. We were totally devastated by his passing as it was so very sudden. Tom had recovered from being very unwell after a big operation as he had to have his thyroid removed only three months before. We shed endless tears for our dream boy. I wished he had never had to go through it all, only to pass three months later, it was tragic. Sitting here writing this I remember one of our biggest happy memories; it was when we let Tom out for the first time following his adoption. He had been incarcerated in a small cage for so long that he developed bad hips. He was so overjoyed at being free, that he ran and ran around the garden until we lost count! He looked alive and so content, it was heartwarming to see.

If I could give you some advice, I'd say don't hold in your emotions. Talk freely about your pet and to your pet (they are intrinsically entwined in our hearts). Laugh at the funny memories and cry at the sad memories. But most of all be open about them and the love you shared.

If there is one message we would like to say to Tom, it would be; "We love you and miss you and we thank you for letting us into your heart and being a significant part of our lives."

We love you ♥

Oliver

By

Debbie Morcom

Handsome Boss Hogg, as we fondly nick named him. This pine and white kitten entered our lives in May 1998. He had been rehomed from a local vet after he was discovered abandoned and living in a garage with his mum. He was fluffy but a little on the scrawny side. We hadn't set out to have a kitten particularly but Oliver and his mum Maisie came as a twosome and they captured our hearts straight away.

Oliver was like no other pet we had ever had, unbelievably intelligent and wily beyond belief. Trying to outsmart us at every turn, he was a never ending source of entertainment and amusement. Oliver was a great bed companion and would walk the rolling barrel as we turned over in bed he would systematically turn with us without rolling off us. He enriched our lives not daily but hourly with his quest for stealing food.

He hooked left over chicken legs out of the oven and our post Sunday lunch ritual was to shut the roasted meat in the bathroom safely out of his reach.

Oliver would sit outside the door and serenade the meat for hours! We knew there was something very wrong when Boss didn't eat his breakfast. We even tried to tempt him with tuna and his much loved chicken. He cried when we picked him up and so made that hasty journey to the vets. We were not prepared for the news. Not in the least. Dear Oliver had an aggressive tumor and his body was slowly shutting down.

Oliver went to sleep on 11th April 2013. We were left bereft and bewildered as he had shown no indication of illness before his journey to Rainbow Bridge. We shed endless tears for our boy. His absence was huge and we often recall with fondness his bed and food stealing habits. He was a gentleman cat with an imaginary smoking jacket and slippers. The best!

A precious memory I have is when we came down stairs one morning to find a dove in the cat bed. It appeared lifeless and dead by all accounts. I went upstairs to tell my partner and when I returned the dove had moved! It was either playing dead or had been stunned. We named the dove Bambino and gently nursed it until such time as its wing was healed. Oliver was obsessed with Bambino until over a week later when we lifted it back into a tree. Oliver was Bambino's hunting trophy which proved just how gentle and non threatening he was. They ended the week the best of friends and Bambino visited Oliver often in the garden.

If I could say anything to my Oliver now it would be "We love you and miss you and thank you for letting us into your heart and being a significant part of our lives."

We love you Oliver ♥

Maisie

By

Debbie Morcom

Beautiful Quasar Doll, as we fondly nick named her. This two year old feline entered our lives in May 1998. We re-homed her from a local vet after she was discovered abandoned and living in a garage with her kitten Oliver that you have just read about. She was very timid, scared and looking a bit raggedy but we knew from that very first moment that with plenty of love and patience she would be herself again. The search was over ………..that beautiful girl was coming home with us. It was a long road but with nurturing she learnt to trust again. Maisie gave us her unwavering love, licks and sandpaper kisses. She was a devil for bringing in mice and voles and we would spend many an evening trying to capture these small furies. She would lay in wait for hours on end and we have fond memories of her being fixated with an active mole hill for an entire day! Fortunately for both Maisie and the mole, he never surfaced to the top!

In early 2009 Maisie sadly developed kidney disease and was on medicated for this condition. Watching her slowly decline was very difficult for us. We knew once she stopped hunting, she would be entering the last chapter of her life. She became incontinent which upset her, but we would wash her bedding every day and stroke her until she was calm again.

On Maisie's final day with us she came across the garden and we could see that her jaw looked odd, it was hanging down. It was clear that she was distressed and in pain. We were filled with dread and panic. We were frightened. The drive to the vets was indescribable. When we went into the treatment room we knew. We just knew. Our sobs filled the building no doubt, especially so, when we sang to her, her special song. "Maisie, Maisie, give me your answer true. I'm half crazy all for the love of you. La la la la la la lala, la la la la la lala……" Maisie Quasar was put to sleep on 16th July 2010. The light in those eyes so wise and knowing where dimmed. We went home with an empty cat bed. We were grieving for our girl. Our first loss of a dear pet as a couple and it was awful. We cried privately and together for months. Our greatest comfort was that we had Oliver. Her boy kitten, which we re-homed with Maisie all those years before.

A memory I cherish, was when within days of bringing both Maisie and Oliver home to live with us, Maisie escaped through an open window. She did not accept her short term captivity. We searched for her high and low for hours on end, calling out her name in the hope that she would come home. It was the hungry cries of her dear kitten Oliver that brought his mummy home. Although hiding, she clearly hadn't gone far and finally came back in after we left the door ajar. That is our happy memory. She came back!

If there was one thing I would say to Maisie, it would be; "We love you and miss you and we thank you for letting us into your heart and being a significant part of our lives". We love you Maisie ♥

Teddy

By

Nicki Huges

Having lost a rescued Ruby Cavalier some years previously, I had always wanted another; I love the colours in their coats (the sun brings out all the different shades of chestnut) and their characters, they seem to be naughtier than other Cavalier colours!

I found someone whom was supposed to be a respected breeder (and Champion Show Judge), they had a young dog (nineteen months) they were looking to re-home. It was Teddy. At the time we had two poorly Cavaliers, so particularly expressed that we were looking for a healthy dog, and knew that a puppy would be too much for the other two, so Teddy seemed perfect. I fell in love with him at first sight; he was such a handsome dog. He had been living in outside kennels but very quickly took to living indoors, loved all the attention and especially toys, particularly his cuddly bear and tennis balls.

Teddy was my heart dog, he always wanted to be with me and would go over any fence or gate to get to me.

I became very attached to him. Teddy used to twirl with excitement; I loved to see his joy for life. He especially loved his walks, and chasing a tennis ball!

His favourite trick was to wipe both paws together over his face, which we called "the cute thing", he would do it on command too, I'm sure he knew it made me go weak at the knees! Teddy loved his cuddles, but when it became too uncomfortable for him to be picked up, he used to lie across my lap so that we could still be close. He found comfort in being close to me. Teddy was already showing symptoms of CM/SM (syringomyelia) when he came to live with us, the breeder said he was recovering from ear infections.

The following year he underwent an MRI scan, which confirmed the diagnosis and sadly from then on it was an emotional roller-coaster, managing his pain and ensuring he still had a good quality of life. It was devastating that such a loving, gorgeous dog should have to suffer with this horrid condition, the only comfort was that he was with us, we knew about it and he received the appropriate veterinary attention. It also meant that we developed a very close bond. I felt so guilty for having had him euthanized but knew it was the kindest action, as his pain could no longer be controlled. I felt that he (and we) had been cheated out of many years together; he was only 6 and should have had much more time with us. It was like losing a part of me. I have a memory from after he left us, it's very special:

I was walking my other Cavaliers on the beach five months after Teddy died; it was a walk we took a few times a week. It's a very quiet location, we would rarely see more than one other person, but usually lots of seals, there is a large resident population of Grey Seals. It was glorious in the sunshine, so I sat on some rocks right next to the sea, and could hear a "pipping" noise. I was looking around for a bird, but couldn't see one. Suddenly a young Otter appeared out of the sea, literally about three feet from me!

The dogs were with me so it went back in to the sea again, but didn't disappear, which I thought was odd. The dogs went off playing and from behind me appeared a female otter. It was her pipping, calling the youngster. The little one came out of the sea again and the two disappeared into the weed. I moved a distance away and watched them for a few minutes before they went back into the sea. What a magical experience! We have seen otters on a few occasions over the years since living here but never so close, and it's the first time I've heard them vocalising.

It would have been Teddy's 7th birthday that day and I was thinking about him and missing him terribly. I think this was his way of letting me know he was thinking of me too? It never gets any easier losing a beloved companion, the dreadful raw pain eases, but you retain sadness that they are no longer with you. You always carry them in your heart, and we are blessed to have shared our lives with them.

I would say to Teddy "If you had your life to live over again, next time I would find you sooner so that I could love you longer. I will always love you; I hope that one day we will be together again."

I love you ♥

Boudica

By

Laksmi Bruce

We took several years to decide we were able to commit to getting a kitten and decided to get two to keep one another company. We decided to get two females, one black and one tabby which we found advertised online. We made arrangements to collect them and bought all the equipment ready for when we brought them home.

When we arrived to collect them, they were black and white and tabby and white but we fell in love with them immediately and weren't going to reject them based on the colour of their fur so we took them home and got them settled in. It also later transpired that the tabby and white kitten was a male so not what we had planned at all!

They gave me an overwhelming feeling of unconditional love and joy, someone to nurture.
They had a huge impact on my life. Looking after another being was something I took it very seriously which is why I waited so long to make the commitment.

I needed to be sure I could provide for them and adjust my life to always put them first. Having them in my life has been the greatest reward I could ever have and has enriched my life tremendously. During dark times in my life, they were my reason to get up in the morning. Watching them thrive and their characters develop has been a privilege. Boudica (black and white female) was very confident from the start and was highly intelligent. The morning after we brought them home, she boldly trotted out of her igloo to explore and, when they were old enough to go outside, she was the one climbing trees that were three storeys high and frightening me to death! An avid hunter, she was a daredevil, a real adrenaline junkie. She was so vibrant and in tune with her body and surroundings. A very beautiful and loving soul but also very strong willed and determined. We were so blessed to have her in our lives for almost ten years.

It was a Thursday night around 7pm and she went out after her evening meal and never returned. It was unusual for her to be out any length of time and not be in the garden so, couple of hours later, my husband went out to search for her but there was no sign. I went out periodically throughout the night to look for her as I couldn't settle but nothing. By morning I was quite distressed so put a notice on social media while I waiting to phone the local vets and the microchip company. As soon as I was able, I made the calls but nothing had been reported. I then got a message on social media requesting me to call somebody with information. My heart sank as I knew it wasn't good news. I felt sick as I called the lady who informed me that, a cat that matched her photograph had been in an RTA around the corner from our home around 7.30pm.

She said she was walking her dog and some people had kindly stopped to tend to her but that she had already passed away and that she didn't know what they had done with her body. I was devastated and my husband had lost his father only four days before We then set out to try and find her body so were looking in bins and asking the local shopkeepers if they had any information but they had all been closed at the time. We just wanted her home. I then got a call from the microchip company who gave me the details of who had scanned her and had her body. They were very nice and brought her back so we could take her to the vets for cremation. We took some comfort that we had her back home and that people had cared enough to treat her with respect and not just discarded her body. We also later found out that the person that found her thought she was asleep as she looked so peaceful. I was absolutely devastated when she passed to the Rainbow Bridge. I knew she would be fine and happy there and that I would see her again but was heartbroken that she was no longer in our physical lives. She's left a huge gap and we miss her terribly every day, especially her brother, Timo. I felt guilty that I couldn't protect her and wondered if she'd been in pain before she passed. It's been ten months since her passing and the tears have lessened as we fondly remember her antics. We know she is only a thought away and she visits us often, we can feel her presence. I know she is with me now as I write this.

One of our fondest memories is when she was a tiny kitten, before they were allowed outside at eight months old. Her brother, Timo, was in the hallway staring at the coats that were hung up. They were rustling then all of a sudden, her little head popped out of the top! It was the beginning of her climbing career! He then tried to copy her but the coats slipped down on top of him as he was a lot bigger which she was highly amused at. She would always outsmart him and she loved it!

The advice I would give to someone experiencing pet loss would be to remember that you did all you could to care for and protect them. Remember they are only a thought away and they remain connected to you always.
Don't feel silly for being upset about their loss. It doesn't matter what anyone else thinks. Think about the wonderful memories and the love you will always share. Know they are still around you and you will be reunited.

If I had the opportunity to speak to her again, I would tell her "we all love you beyond space and time and we miss you every day. Thank you for making me a better person and teaching me unconditional love and that I look forward to being reunited with you in the spirit world someday."

We love you Boudica ♥

Dudley

By

Lisa Walker

Dudley arrived in our lives in 2002, I had made several enquiries about a Bedlington terrier and he was one of the few puppies available at the time. We flew from our home in Hertfordshire, England to Scotland to get him.

When we arrived at the kennels, we didn't meet him for a good half an hour as the breeder was chatting so much! When we eventually got to his cage, he didn't rush over, just sat there being shy with a lopsided sit. We picked up a hire car and began our long drive home, he was very quiet and I couldn't believe we had our very own puppy. We stopped for petrol on route and at this point he was on my lap.

Something startled him whilst my husband was putting petrol in the car and he rushed up at my face scratching me. He was a hard puppy to settle, he had to sleep in our room and have the works, toys, blankets, a ticking clock and a rigid routine.

Eventually he settled and the next Bedlington puppy, a sister called Dafni was comforted and licked to death by him constantly; he was the perfect puppy sitter. He needed a tight rein and could be quite will full, but was a kind, gentle dog with all people and dogs that he met. If anything, he could be shy and hide behind your legs when strangers approached.

When our son was first born, I lost Dudley in the house one day, only to find him sat at the foot of his Moses basket keeping guard. He suffered in life with his skin as he got older and eventually had to have injections to calm his system down every few months. As time went on he developed congestive heart failure and this took more of a hold as he got over the age of eleven. At thirteen years and a few months, he began to decline, he had one last Norfolk camping holiday with us that summer, but by December was having some bad nights.

On 23rd December 2015, he paced all day, retched, coughed and couldn't get his breath. He sat with the kids in the lounge, but by early evening he made his way to his bed to lie down and die. I prayed it would be a quick passing and it was, with all of us around him. I will remember him most for the beautiful coat he possessed and the way his trotted along like a show dog with a perfect gait, and for his last summer camping holiday with us where he rallied and had a great time. Unfortunately, we all know that pet loss is a certainty, I feel what matters is the life and experiences we give them and how we can make a difference to their lives. They never really leave us and we must keep them in our thoughts but also allow them to pass to the higher realms that they need to. After Dudley passed, we continued, for a while, to hear his back door "let me in" barking. I knew it was his way of letting us know he was still watching. It stopped when I told him it was ok for him to go when he wanted to.

If I could chat with Dudley now, I would thank him for his unwavering affection and watchfulness through all his nearly fourteen years with us and all of the family challenges he lived through.

We love you Dudley ♥

Morrigan

By

Vicky Moore

I got Morrigan from the Cats Protection shelter in Milton Keynes in May 2003. We went to the shelter looking for an older cat that would be happy to live only indoors, as the location of our flat meant that it would not have been safe for a cat to go outside there. We were told that she was the only cat who was suitable for our requirements, and we were introduced to her. My first memory of her is a big black cat in a shelter pen, looking nervous and quite stand-offish. Her name at the time was Brownie, which totally didn't suit her as she was black! After we met her for the first time, my husband and I went out for dinner to discuss her, and I knew she was meant to be ours, and that I would change her name to Morrigan (the name of a Celtic Goddess).

We had another meeting with Cats Protection and they came to assess our flat, and once we passed the assessment we were able to go and pick her up.

She came from the shelter with her own comb, which she was very attached to as she loved to be groomed! There is no question that Morrigan was a 'difficult' cat to begin with.

She was around eight years old, when she came to us and from what we were told about her history, it sounded as though she had had a hard life, being moved from owner to owner, and eventually having to be split up even from her own sister as they didn't get along.

For the first couple of months that we had her, we had to keep her confined only to the bathroom and kitchen in our flat, otherwise she would just disappear and hide under the bed, so we couldn't make sure she was eating, drinking, and using her tray properly. As she (very slowly!) came out of her shell and started to trust us, we were able to allow her into the lounge, and eventually into the bedroom as well, and then she was able to have the run of the flat at all times. The change in her was amazing, and that is one of the fondest memories I have that we were able to work with her to slowly make her relax and trust us. She was always nervous with people she didn't know, but with us she was incredibly affectionate. I only had to get her comb out and she would come running over and jump onto my lap to be groomed.

The day I found out I was going to lose her was one of the worst of my life. For several years Morrigan had suffered bouts of vomiting, but every time we took her to the vet they just blamed her age, or said it was 'just one of those things that some cats did'.

In January 2011, though, she had another bout and it was the worst ever, she would not eat or drink at all, so I took her back to the vet again on the Monday. This time the vet remarked on a smell that she had, which I had noticed on and off when she had been ill previously. He said that this was a sign of kidney failure in cats, so he decided to give her a blood test.

I took her home, and that evening the vet phoned with the terrible news, the test had shown that she had kidney failure, which was so severe that she had barely any kidney function left. He advised that we needed to have her put to sleep that week, but said it didn't have to be immediate as she wasn't suffering. I made the appointment for her to be put to sleep on the Wednesday evening. I had to work on the Tuesday but my intention was to spend the whole day with her on the Wednesday, so that her last day would be as happy as I could make it. However, it was not to be. When I got home from work on the Tuesday, she was restless and seemed distressed. I phoned the vet to see if she could be given painkillers or any drugs to keep her comfortable, but he said there was nothing that would help. We tried to hang on, but I couldn't leave her like that for another day, so we had to take her to the vet late that night, where she was sadly put to sleep. The vet who did it said that she did not look like a cat with kidney failure, as she was still so sleek and beautiful, and he said we must have looked after her very well. After she had passed away, we sent her to be cremated and her ashes are now in a wooden casket which I keep on the mantel shelf with a photo of her.

Morrigan's passing left me heartbroken. The first morning after she had been put to sleep was so hard, because my morning routine was centred around feeding her, and it just hit me so hard that I no longer had that to do. I took all the food, litter etc that we still had for her to the Cats Protection, as it was too difficult to keep it in the house, but I kept her comb and I still have it today. It took me a very long time to recover from her passing, and even after we got a new kitten in May of that year, I was still grieving. I eventually had to have some counselling to help me come to terms with it, and to this day there are times when I miss her terribly, and still have feelings of guilt. I often wonder, could I have done something different? Even though logically I know there was nothing I could have done.

One of the best memories I have of Morrigan is of how she coped with our move from Milton Keynes to York in 2008.

Because she was always such a nervous cat, I had no idea how she would cope with such a long journey, and I even considered asking Cats Protection to take her back, so she didn't have to go through that. But in the end, she handled it amazingly well, she was calm in her carrier as we travelled up the motorways, and when we brought her into the new flat, she was confident and curious, and perfectly happy. The flat in York had huge windows so always got the sun, and she loved sitting in the sunny spots. I felt so proud of how much she had changed from the nervous cat who hid behind the toilet when we first had her!

The piece of advice I would give to anyone who has experienced pet loss is simply; give yourself time to grieve, acknowledge your feelings, and don't be ashamed to get professional help from a counsellor if you need it.

If I could say one thing to Morrigan, it would simply be to tell her "I love you so much, and to thank her you for being my soul mate for the eight years, you were in my life.

I will always love you Morrigan ♥

Buster

By

Sonia Turner

Buster was a surprise early Christmas present for me from my boyfriend on the 21st December 2001. That was the day Buster entered my life. I had never owned a dog before but we bonded instantly. My boyfriend at the time came through the front door with a tiny brown bewildered puppy in his arms, I knew instantly he was mine, "the breeder called him Buster" he said, I took Buster into my arms and he snuggled his little puppy head into the left side of my neck and paws either side. My heart melted and our bond was sealed

Buster was a Staffordshire bull terrier and I was totally unaware of the awful reputation that these dogs had. It soon became apparent to me that this was the reason that people would look down their nose at me or cross the road to avoid us. How anyone could be scared of these beautiful dogs was beyond me, they were nick named as the 'Nanny Dog' but at the same time they were used for dog fights. I was appalled by what I was learning, and over the years because of Buster, something had changed inside me.

I am now on a committee of a Staffy Rescue saving dogs lives that are not as lucky as Buster was.

Buster made me laugh every day with his funny little ways, when he wanted something he would sit in front of me with one ear bolt upright, he was the most impatient dog I ever met and stubborn! He would NEVER give in until he got what he wanted, even if it meant waiting an hour until his dinner time arrived. Whilst out on walks he would run to the grass and do a dramatic roll on the arrival. He never begged for food unless I was cooking Spaghetti Bolognese, then he would sit in the kitchen with me 'helping'. When getting his food ready, Buster would stand on the right side of me with his left paw firmly on my right foot as if to keep me in place until I was ready to give it to him! He was scared of the buzzer in Family Fortunes and the theme tune to 'You've Been Framed'.

As Buster got older he hated the text alert on my mobile phone so I had to change that, if I sneezed or coughed he would walk out of the room. Buster wasn't a cuddly dog at all, if I tried to cuddle him he would walk away, he was very independent but very happy to know I was around for company. When Buster did want cuddles it was very special knowing it came from him and not because I asked him. All of these funny little ways he had made me love him all the more. As Buster got older his health deteriorated, at the age of ten years he was diagnosed with an under active Thyroid which was managed with medication, at twelve years he became very poorly with pancreatitis and peritonitis, the specialist said he had fifty percent chance of survival, as soon as she said that and knowing Busters stubbornness I knew he would make a full recovery!

The last year of Busters life he suffered with neurological problems and his back legs got very weak, I got him a buggy to push him around in but Buster being stubborn hated it!

So, we just did lots of short gentle walks and car rides.

As time went on I knew I had to make the awful decision was looming. Buster was struggling to walk but his mind seemed all intact, I hated being the one that would decide when his life was over, I begged him to go in his sleep and I would know it was when he was ready. I spoke to my vet lots of times and she was fantastic with me, she promised she would tell me when it was the right time and told me that Buster was very lucky to have an owner that became his carer.

One morning something had changed in Buster, he couldn't stand for more than 10 seconds, I rang my vet and she said to bring him in that evening so she would check him over. I just knew that this was THE day, I cried privately away from Buster and stayed strong in front of him, he just slept most of the day apart from the couple of times I carried him to the garden to go to the loo or to his water bowl for a drink. We arrived at the vets, we waited with Buster in the car until the vet was ready to see us, she came out to the car, I got him out and he was struggling to stand, she looked him over, put her hand on my shoulder and gently said to me "I think it is his time". I just nodded with silent tears rolling down my cheeks.

My Husband carried Buster into the vets and the vet sedated him giving us some time to say our goodbyes. I asked the vet if I could hold Buster in my arms as he made his journey over Rainbow Bridge, I wanted to hold him the same way as he entered my life with his head snuggled into the left side of my neck and paws either side. This was the worst day of my life 16th June 2016. I felt so empty, the biggest part of my life for the last fourteen and a half years had gone, I concentrated so much on looking after Buster in his final months, making sure he didn't suffer and the time was right that I didn't even stop to think how I would cope when he had gone. Empty is the only word I can use to describe it.

For weeks coughing or sneezing felt weird, not having to keep them suppressed so I didn't frighten Buster.

I avoided people because I knew they would all ask after him. I had Buster cremated the next day and bought his ashes home that evening, I have some fur clippings, and his left paw print which is now tattooed on my right foot. His ashes are in a Staffordshire bull terrier urn with his collar and tag around its neck, fresh flowers and a candle I light at night for him.

I have so many happy memories of Buster but one of many that stick in my mind and makes me smile would be trying to sneak tablets into Busters food, he had the ability to find it and spit it out, sometimes across the room but still manage to eat the food it was concealed in without dropping any of it.

One piece of advice I would give to others about pet loss is cry when you are sad, don't bottle it up, look at photos and smile away the sad tears.

If I could just say anything to Buster it would be "Thank-you for fourteen and a half years of happiness, I hope I haven't let you down in anyway and that I did everything I could to be the best Mummy to you and I love you more than I can put into words

I love you Buster ♥

Jack

By

Diane Beck

Jack and I first met because he was locally wandering as a big stray ginger tom and was known to the locals as the stray ginger tom. He had a little wounded friend that he also used to hang around with and look after. We would see the two of them together. They used to sleep on warm engines under cars and on wheels.

It was winter and it was snowing and one night I looked out at a willow tree opposite my front window on a small green and saw Jack sat under the tree in the snow. It was freezing. I just couldn't allow him to keep sleeping out in the winter cold. I wanted to help him. I called a local cat home and the RSPCA. They told me they would catch him and his friend to neuter and flea them, but couldn't keep them both as local catteries were full. I said I would look after them as outdoor cats after they were neutered and that they could be caught and left in my garden.

The night before they were caught, I played music and opened the patio door, both cats sniffed the air listening to music and looked thankful I was feeding them and talking to them, especially playing music for them; it was very beautiful to watch.

Jack was very friendly; desperate to befriend anyone that would stroke him, but didn't like being asked to come into the house, staying outside at this point was fine for him. When both cats were caught and neutered I received a call telling me that the small black and white cat had feline HIV and they advised to put him to sleep which was so very sad.

Jack however, was healthy. He was left in my garden and I saw him stumbling, post operation. I immediately picked him up and brought him in, woozy from his operation. It was love. I really fell for him. This enormous gentle ginger tom, stumbling with post operation drugs and needing comfort was in my home. He didn't like being shut in though, but for his safety, I kept him in, prepared a bed and food and water and told my partner that we had a visitor for the night.

The next day I had to introduce him to the house. I will never forget the first time he saw a bed and duvet. He looked so gentle and excited to see a bed. From then on, he was out pet. He loved sleeping in cardboard boxes regardless of expensive beds, he loved cardboard boxes under the radiator and every morning I would wake with him staring at me. He'd lay on my chest with a paw by my ears. He was amazing. He seemed to be the top cat in the area with cat friends and a tough stray attitude and a baby boy cuddle attitude at home.

One day the boy next door who had been in a domestic fight with one of his parents knocked on our door in tears. Jack was amazing with children, he jumped next to the boy and lay with him to comfort him. He was a wonderful healing boy.

The little boy loved him and was surprised that the cat seemed to be looking after him. He cheered me up and was very close. He brought love and fun into the house as pets always do. I then couldn't imagine a house without him. He was very protective of me and was sleeping by me on the floor every night in his box.

One fond memory was watching him box another cat while literally up on his hind legs whilst using his front paws to stop a cat trying to bully him. Another was waking up with his arms by my head, or the first time he saw a duvet and he started to purr at the very sight of it.

There were many lovely memories, he was just so special. He would look into my eyes like he was communicating long messages.

He loved children, he was sensitive and so grateful for his home. He was my soft furred, ginger prince. Unfortunately, he became ill and he would sit under the bed, quiet. I was to and fro to the vets and they told me they didn't know what was wrong with him, pumping him with pain killers. Jack was crying in pain and I was nursing him. The vet still didn't identify what the problem was. Finally, after he was really upset, we went back to the vet practice, luckily, we saw a new vet, who found a lump in Jack, so he was immediately operated on. I went to work expecting a call that day with an update, unfortunately though, they were advising me not to wake him from the operation. I didn't get a chance to say good bye. The vet had given me a squeeze when they took him from me to the operating room, as if assuring me it was just another routine operation and it was just to see what the problem was. I knew Jack didn't want me to go, it was so upsetting but I trusted the vet.

Hearing the news, he was going to be euthanized was devastating. It took me a week off work to get over it. Id nursed him for so long and hoped it may be somehow solvable.

But my beloved, gorgeous, dependable, soul mate cat Jack had gone. The feelings of loss were immense. I cried a lot and I felt it hit me so hard, like losing a close relative. I'd never grieved for a pet that way, but I did with Jack because of the close bond we shared, he also seemed dependent on me and bonded in a way I felt responsible. I was exhausted with grief. I took a week off, slept a lot, cried a lot and then we decided to honour the invitation to other stray cats in his name. My partner was also devastated, He missed him terribly.

A memory I have with Jack was him waiting till my partner went to work in the morning and then curling up next to me on the other side of the bed and rolling over on his back. He liked to lay with his legs akimbo on his back and his paws daintily in the air. My beautiful funny boy!

My advice to others who have lost a pet is, remember them and continue the love and communicate with them. They may have passed over but the energy bond is still there. They teach us so much.

One thing I would like to say to Jack is "I love you. I am sorry I didn't realise how much pain you were in! If I'd have known it was that serious, I would have tried to help you sooner. I am sad that they didn't allow me a long goodbye that final time; in fact, they pulled you from me thinking it was just a routine operation and I was so sad that I didn't get to comfort you and be with you. I love you. You warmed my heart and helped me through a lot of tough times. I miss you and think about you often. The other cats we opened the door to after you, were because of you."

I love you Jack you're in my heart forever.♥

Max

By

Carolyn Hutchins

Max, aka Maximus Mischief Maker

Max came into our lives on a late November night in 2010. He was the youngest of three pups to our two other Border Terriers Alfie & Daisymae.

My first memory of Max was hearing the most heart wrenching scream coming from one of the rooms in a veterinary college; we thought a cat had been knocked over. According to a nurse, some over exuberance by his mum when tearing his bag off during birth, accidently led to her slitting his mouth either side. He looked like the joker, but we weren't convinced. Thrust into my husband's hands by a nurse we were told there was no hope for him. He was cold, lifeless and his whimpers of pain broke our hearts. My husband told me to open my fleece and put him close to me to warm him up, that's where he spent the first hour of his life next to my heart. So, with mum making her way to the exit she wasn't hanging around and our makeshift incubator with two other pups in, we set off to sort our little boy out.

Unable to latch onto mum we spent over a week hand feeding him until he was able to latch on to her. Every day he stole a piece of my heart he was the most beautiful courageous funny boy.

He was such a loving boy his zest for life was just amazing, just watching him made me smile. His favourite toy was of all things a yoghurt pot, spending many an hour running around the garden throwing it in the air, goading anyone to play with him or just playing on his own. He loved to watch animal programs, especially the meerkats, monkeys were also his favourite. Oh, and dogs, he even tried to sniff the screen on many occasions. Just to look at Max would make your heart melt.

My fondest memory of Max was on a holiday in Devon and his first time on a beach. He did zoomies in big circles and then would just stop dead in front of us as though to say "look mum it's the seaside why aren't you excited". He always stayed close to Daisymae and was very protective over her; it was a joy seeing them together. He was my shadow he would be in the kitchen when I cooked, and he would jump up standing on the washing machine door. He was chief taster and he loved to sit with you when watching TV, that's when he wasn't right up the front of the TV! He just loved to be with you.

Max started to have fits in early march 2016 for over a week. A month later they came back for over a week, they got worse and on the Friday they said he may be epileptic and started him on medication. Over the weekend, he just got worse. Every time he had a fit we lost a part of him, it was heart-breaking.

And on the Sunday before he died he lay in my arms with his head on my chest like when he was a baby and looked at me as though to say "I've had enough mum".

We took him back to the vet and they said he was dehydrated and would keep him in, they would put him on a drip and monitor him, and would call us in the morning. I called them twice that evening, I was so worried.

The second time I called, they said he was brighter and sitting up, so I thought my beautiful boy will be home soon. The following day at 6.45am we got the phone call that would change everything; we never thought we would be told that our boy had gone. They told us he was brighter, so they took him for a walk and he was put back in his crate afterwards. They went back five minutes later to check on him and he had passed away. The pain of losing my boy is one of the most horrible pains I've ever known. You know that they have to leave you one day, but you're never really prepared. I've lost my best friend, my shadow. My Max who could always make me smile would lick away my tears, whose love just flowed from him and who spoke to me with his eyes. He was so full of life, how could my boy be gone? he was just too young, he had so much more to give. Watching max play, running in and out of the garden with his yogurt pot or plastic plant pot he'd found amidst of garden stuff, the mayhem of the others playing, him just making his own noise joining in but playing his own game. I miss it all. He loved being with his mum, dad, and brothers when they come to visit, it was like being a puppy all over again, in fact, I don't think he ever stopped being one, I just loved watching him.

My advice to you would be to just allow yourself to grieve in your own way, they are not 'just a dog or cat' they are part of your family! They leave a massive whole that can't be filled. They give so much unconditional love and loyalty that they just want to be loved back.

Talk to them and talk about them don't ever forget them. If I could tell Max one last thing it would be "I love you with all my heart, you were not just a dog, you were my friend, my buddy.

I'm sorry I couldn't stop you being scared of big black dogs, but I hope I made you feel safe and you knew I wouldn't let anyone or anything hurt you. I miss you so much. I love you Max to the moon and stars and back. You are always in my thoughts and forever in my heart, sleep tight sweetheart you are so loved and missed."

I love you Max ♥

Banjo

By

Lara Cartwright

Banjo came into my life at a time when I needed him more than I ever realised, we were so attuned he was my soul mate. He was a home bred boy and I knew from the moment I saw him that he was going to be with me, even when someone else took a shine to him, I knew he'd be staying with me

As he grew in those first few weeks it was quite apparent that this boy was echoing my own traits, he was happiest when he was sat on the sidelines , watching his siblings shenanigans, independent and aloof if he considered you a friend he was beside himself with giddiness to see you and would love you to the ends of the earth but if you weren't in that small circle of chosen friends he wouldn't as much as give you the time of day and his signature move was to turn his back to you.

He could read me better than most humans, he became my clown when I was sad, my protector when I needed it and my confidence to face the world through some pretty tough times. The love I had for this boy was and still is immense, way beyond measure. Banjo became my confidence, he came into my life when I was at a low ebb, from amongst other things a relationship break up, he was a focus for me and soon became almost my guide dog, guiding me through life. I don't cope with people at the best of times & he became a focus of positive experiences with people because of his sheer size and at the time the fact that Leonbergers were rarely seen, he caught people's attention and they were inquisitive. So when I developed a severe case of rosacea he was the focus and not my severely pitted bright red face, without him by my side Id have become a true hermit, I had a lot of negative rude experiences, people would stare, laugh, whisper, even walk round an aisle in the supermarket to come and have another stare at the freak that was me and my severely affected face and I would become so stressed, but with him, I was calmer and people would focus on him and be nice about my rosacea if they mentioned it at all

Banjo was my world, he knew that he could make me smile with his quirky ways, he was as stubborn as an ox at times, he would vocally tell me off and nudge me if I ever had to leave him at home and nibble my bum if he was really cross with me. He'd then ignore me for a while.

He would go to bed early at night and pace till I came upstairs, if I took a long time he'd 'shout' down to me from the top of the stairs, he was like a little old man at times, you would say he was eccentric with his little ways, but I wouldn't change his character for the world, I miss him with all my heart Banjo was afflicted with several conditions and had a rough ride on the road to diagnosis with a few misdiagnoses that potentially could have taken him from me much sooner due to unnecessary meds.

Thank fully he went to see a specialist in Cambridge (Queens Veterinary College) who quickly got him off the dangerous meds, but gave us the devastating news that Banjo not only had Laryngeal Paralysis but Polyneuropathy too!

Through being my rock and all the upset & stress, I firmly believe this was the cause of his Colitis and we had many little flare ups which he would bounce back from within at most forty-eight hours.

In Sept of 2010 I'd started to take a serious interest in photography & one weekend I was asked if I'd like to go and watch and take photos at a motocross event in Cambridgeshire that my Nephew was competing in. I agreed to go, but just a few days prior, Banjo started with his Colitis and this time it seemed persistent, so I was dubious about leaving him. My family reassured me that if he got any worse they would let me know so to go and enjoy myself. I remember vividly the feeling of being unsettled the first night & morning, I rang home to be told he's ok but I still couldn't shake the feeling or keep the boy out of my thoughts, I rang & messaged home numerous times that weekend to be told the same thing. By the Sunday afternoon I just couldn't wait to get home, my eldest nephew asked me why I was sad and I remember saying, "I just know that Banjo's more poorly than I'm being told and I need to get to him", It was a long wait for the racing to finish and even longer drive home

When I got home, my usual greeting at the gate of being told off vocally for leaving him and bottom nibble wasn't there and my heart sank, I entered the house to find my boy very quiet, laid on his bed and not even a wag of the tail, I was gutted, he'd been there for me so many times and when he needed me the most, I'd selfishly left him to go off and supposedly 'enjoy' myself, something that still haunts me to this day.

Banjo was really ill for about two weeks after I came home that weekend from motocross, I took him to the vets on the Monday and he was initially treated for his Colitis, he perked up but little signs were there that it was much more than colitis but I wasn't ready to give up on him.

We were at the vets several times over that fortnight for checkups and there'd be little signs that would give hope.

I couldn't let go just yet, but then, on return from one visit from the vets he refused to get out of the car, he spent several hours just laid in the back on his bed, and nothing could encourage him to get out. I looked into his eyes and it was then I knew we weren't going to beat this, he'd truly had enough, I knew in my heart that he'd fought to keep going until I was ready to accept it was his time and he could fight any longer, for a fortnight he'd pushed himself and that day in the car, I finally gave in & accepted I could do no more and my boy needed his rest. He finally came in from the car albeit reluctantly.

That night as I lay with him, I told him it was ok, I knew I had to stop being selfish & he had to do what was right for him, I'd cope and it was time to go and be with his friends, mum & dad who'd gone before him, it was the hardest conversation I had with him. After a lot of unnecessary upset by a very aggressive vet making the situation much more traumatic than it should have been, arrangements were made and I must say, given the events leading up to his passing, with his last breath, Banjo curled his lip at the vet as she checked him over and I knew he was still aware up to the very end and tried to protect me from the upset she had added to an already traumatic situation.

I was heartbroken, lost and totally beside myself at losing my boy, I sank into depression and struggled without my four-legged warrior, I wanted and did shut the world out.

I felt so guilty for not being there that weekend he took poorly and for being so selfish that he pushed himself for a fortnight as he knew he couldn't let go until I was ready

A memory I treasure was from the only holiday we went on, it was to Bournemouth with my Sister, we took Banjo's brother who lived with my sister and my Newfoundland (who came to us when Banjo was five years Old)

We decided to take a trip to Stonehenge, it was midweek and we were surprised at how busy it was, we also soon realised that no dogs were allowed on the Stonehenge site, so as we walked back to the car with two Leonbergers and a Newfoundland, we found ourselves being stopped for cuddles, photos and little chats and for nearly an hour with each new coach of people that arrived, we became more of an attraction than Stonehenge itself! I was so proud of how all three coped with all the attention and in particular my aloof boy Banjo.

On another occasion, I remember with much love was our attempt at showing, it was an important show for the breed as it was the first time CCs were awarded and as such a very knowledgeable judge from Italy had been invited, at this point I have to say Banjo who got bored easily and if he didn't want to do something, well he would either be a complete clown or glue his feet to the floor and refuse to move!

Our class came up and off we went , in line, stacking & trying to make it look as though we knew what we were doing, group movement went ok, back to waiting to be given the once over which went well, then our individual movement, our spotlight moment.

Nervous and not wanting to trip up or fall over, we set off, a few steps in and I felt a nudge, a nibble, yep I had a clown on my hands and my goodness how embarrassed was.

I had this bouncing spring lamb at the end of the lead, I looked round to see the judges reaction and the potential glares from the experienced owners, but I was relieved to see the judge chuckling, he called me back to start again and said with a big smile. "You are both new to this yes?" Phew, "yes I'm so sorry" and off we went again, still being a spring lamb and nudging me but we got around and needless to say that was the end of our show career. My advice to others grieving the loss of a pet is let your grief take its course, don't let others dictate how long you grieve; everyone's path through grief is different.

I don't care what people say when they say it was just a dog (in my case) I'm grieving not only a family member, but my best friend and soul mate & for me it doesn't get easier. I've just learnt the coping strategies, there will still be tears and sadness, but eventually happy tears will outweigh the sad tears, but remember sad tears are still allowed too.

I love you Banjo ♥

Lucky

By

Beth Hanley

It was during early summer when I went outside on the farm that I lived on and heard meowing. I looked around and found the tiniest sweetest little fluffball of a kitten and it was wandering through the grass. The grass was taller than he was, so it must have seemed like a huge scary jungle to such a tiny wee thing. He was so very small and young, I guesstimated his age to be around four to five weeks old. I also soon located his siblings. I am a sucker for baby animals, so my heart was exploding with love for them, but I couldn't keep them all. I got them to where they were weaned and found homes for them. I had decided to keep the one with the biggest brightest eyes and the white on his upper lips was so white, it looked like they were standing out in a comical and adorable way.

He got his name as he got injured the same day when he went under the reclining chair that the foot piece was out and my youngest son leaned on it and when it came down it hit him in the back.

He lost the use of his rear legs. I was devastated watching him drag them behind him and cry. I took him to the vet, to which nothing could be determined. They told me to wait over the weekend, perhaps swelling would go down and he would regain the use of his legs. If not, he would have to be put down. He ended up being all right and so I aptly named him Lucky. Well being so small and adorable was all it took. We are all cat lovers and he soon found himself adored. He loved everyone in our family. He loved to give hugs and head rubs and show his love. His heart was huge but he would run and hide when strangers came over.

Later on, when I moved to where I currently live he attached himself very strongly to my daughter, Aspen, who is now fifteen. She grew up with him all of her life. He was two when she was born and he was always very curious about her. He had become so bonded with Aspen and knew her moods and could detect when she was having an anxiety episode or getting depressed and would be there for her with hugs and more love. He would allow her to hug him tight and cry into his fur with never trying to escape her grasp, instead he would melt into her and be there. He heard her many secrets and wishes and her joys and sorrows. He was her emotional support. I didn't know she even had anxiety or depression as Lucky aided her in managing it so well.

He had been having health issues and at the time I wasn't financially able to afford a vet to diagnose him, something I still feel immense guilt over. I never knew what was truly ailing him or if he was in pain. He never seemed to show discomfort. He just kept losing weight and he would sleep more and more and he threw up often. It was Aspen's decision to have him put down even though he had become so important and crucial in her life.

I hated to let him go even though I knew he was suffering saying just give him another day even though I knew it wasn't in his best interest.

Letting him go was so very difficult. But Aspen was firm and said he wants to go to be free of his suffering but he doesn't want to go because we love him so much.

Our neighbour works for a Vet so we contacted him and he made arrangements for her to come to our place. We didn't want Lucky to be all stressed out in a sterile vet's office. If he was to pass away, I wanted him in the comfort of his home surrounded by Aspen and myself hugging him. We told him how much we loved him and would miss him but that it was okay for him to go. After we said it was okay for him to go, he passed quickly. When the vet took his vitals and told us he was gone Aspen and I totally lost our composure. We were crying, holding onto Lucky, and then to each other. It was a couple of weeks after he had been buried that I was notified by one of my daughter's friends of a suicidal post she made on snapchat. I immediately spoke to Aspen and we then arranged for her to see someone. She was prescribed another emotional support/therapy animal. This time it was a puppy. However, she still misses Lucky as do I. Lucky was buried in a very special place. It is under an oak tree that is known as a sacred fairy wishing tree.

We were both emotionally destroyed by him not being present in our lives anymore in the physical sense. I harboured great guilt and still do, for not having taken him to the vet to find out what ailed him. Aspen was the one who has suffered most as he was her emotional support and got her through her darkest moments with unconditional love. To lose him was like losing a light in our lives and household. He had such a big heart and was so full of love and in his old age realized that strangers were okay.

Our house just seems empty without him here with us. We both wish we could have him back in our lives. Saying we are still heartbroken is an understatement. I still feel guilt at not having taken him to Vet to be diagnosed and I didn't want him to be mad at me for having him put down.

I honestly just wish I could know what he thinks from the other side and for him to know how much he is missed and loved even now.

For myself I would have to say that his entire life with us was one big happy memory. Every day he showed us such love, huge immense love. Even in his ailing old age he would still get the urge to play like a kitten when provoked with string. I think the best thing was you always knew when he was really happy when his whiskers would stick out in front of him till the tips touched.

For Aspen, it is the fact that he was her best friend. He was there for her in her darkest hours with unconditional love and he also loved to make her laugh by wanting to sit on her shoulders or pouting because she spent night at a friend's so he faked being mad at her until she went over the top in asking his forgiveness. Then he would literally wrap his paws around her neck and hug her so very long and hard and then they would go cuddle for hours.

As for a word of advice: Don't ever forget how much they loved you. They showed it daily in the ways they knew how. To them YOU were their whole world, so remember that with your living animals now, they depend on you for everything, they love you so very much and depend on you for their very existence, cherish them while alive and in death. Never forget them and the gifts that they truly are.

If there was something I could say to Lucky now, it would be: "THANK YOU!! Thank you for letting me be your mom, even with my shortcomings and loving me. For all of those hugs and head bumps, Thank you. Thank You for being there for Aspen, your girl, the human side of yourself whom you loved even more than me, who bottle fed you as a baby. I MISS YOU so VERY much and would so love to be able to hold you just one more time."
(And now I am crying).

Aspen would like to tell you: "Lucky, I love you so much and would do anything to hug and kiss you just one more time. That even though I have Newt my dog, I will never forget you or stop loving you and that you were and are my everything to me!"

Lucky we love you ♥

Ozzy

By

Kelly Kerr

When I contacted a local cat rescue centre in 2003, I was told about a sweet little kitten that was rescued from outside, and looking for her forever home. I just knew this little baby was destined to share my life.

Valentine's Day 2003 arrived and I drove to meet up with the lady from the rescue centre in a car park near to home. I was feeling excited and nervous about the meeting. She brought out this tiny little bundle, wrapped in a blanket. I could see she had very weepy eyes, and looked thin too. Not the bouncy little kitten I'd expected to meet. She said she'd brought another kitten with her, in case I didn't want this one (that sounded an awful thing to say!) She was coming home with me and nothing would change my mind. She needed me, maybe as much as I needed her. I really had found love on Valentine's Day ♡

At home, Ozzy as I decided to call her was absolutely terrified of everything. She began to yowl, as if in terrible pain if you got anywhere close to her. I felt so useless, and hated that she was so frightened of me.

Over the coming weeks though, with patience I tried to build up some trust between us. I knew the road ahead was going to be a long one, but I already loved Ozzy and would do whatever it took to help her. The vet said the reason for her weepy eyes was because she was in the final stages of cat flu, and she also had stomach problems, so the daily eye drops and medication made building her trust even more difficult. Ozzy was such a nervous little cat, so I learned to become more patient and found that my approach to other situations were different since she'd come into my life. I appreciated all the little steps that we made together, such as the first time she decided to come to me and then when she allowed me to stroke her for the very first time. Even those little steps were actually huge achievements, real progress for both of us. I think when you look at your life in this way, and appreciate the little things you don't tend to take so much for granted. I knew that the outside world would have terrified her, so she lived indoors, where she felt safe.

In time, she became quite playful and a favourite game was rolling a ping pong ball back and forth to each other. It amazed me that she actually pawed it right back to me, every time! Clever girl!

My other cat Tigger was still young, so they bonded well and loved snuggling together. Sadly, Tigger passed away when she was just five, and I knew that Ozzy would miss her dearly. During the time, they'd spent together I'm sure Tigger helped her confidence, probably more than I ever could.

As Ozzy became more confident, she decided she liked head bumps. She couldn't cope with being lifted or held in any way, but she could still show love with head bumps.

She accepted our new kitten Saffron, but never wanted to play with her. I think they just learned to accept each other's ways, and just be company for each other.

About a year or so before losing Ozzy, she'd started to do the toilet on the floor. This was something she'd never done. She'd always had stomach problems and ate prescription cat food, but never went outside her litter tray. Sadly, things got worse and she started to lose weight, so we had to visit the vet even though it was traumatic for her. Our vet was so gentle.

After weeks of medication, a change in food and lots of blood tests, there was no improvement, things were getting worse and she lost more weight. She was fading away before us, and it was heart breaking to watch. I knew she needed me to make that awful decision. She didn't have quality of life, and our vet assured me that I was making the right decision.

When the day arrived, I gave Ozzy and Saffron tuna. She didn't get treats because of her stomach, so she had to have something yummy. They stood side by side eating, whilst I cried. My husband and I headed to the vet with Ozzy. I kept going over and over things in my head, worrying about my decision. In my heart though, I knew it was time. She passed very quickly, which confirmed it was the right time. She was twelve and a half. We'd been through so much together, and she always listened to my problems. This was my final gift to her, no matter how difficult.

My way of thanking her for supporting me I was setting her free from the pain and suffering. I kissed her head, said goodnight and told her I loved her. My heart broke the day we said goodbye to Ozzy, and I knew my husband struggled with it too, as they adored each other. I'd only just lost my granny, so the sadness I now felt was unbearable. In the months that followed coming to terms with losing Ozzy was extremely difficult. She'd been with me for a huge part of my adult life, and now everything felt so wrong without her.

I kept expecting her to come walking into the room, or come running towards me when I came downstairs in the morning. Sometimes I'd even forget she was gone, and shout on her. This upset me even more.

As time went on, I was able to accept that I had done what Ozzy needed me to do, and this actually confirmed just how much I loved her. It would have been selfish to allow her to continue suffering, just because I couldn't let go. I loved her too much for that.

When I got together with my husband Ewan in 2011, Ozzy really took to him. She even started to sit on his knee, and allow him to stroke her. She always hid when visitors came to the flat, so it was lovely to see her so confident with him. When I decided to move in with him the following year, I was worried how Ozzy would cope. It was an exciting time, but I also felt extremely anxious about moving her to unknown territory. What if she lost the confidence she'd found or just hated it! I needn't have worried, as it seems it was the best move for Ozzy too. She was happier than she'd ever been, and loved to lie on Ewan's chest when he watched TV. I couldn't believe the change in her, it was as if my happiness made her happy too. She really was a different cat, our beautiful girl had become so brave and even more loving. She adored my step-children, Emily and Harry too. They were always so gentle and patient with her, and she loved them for it. This is my favourite memory of Ozzy as making that move meant she spent her final years in such a happy place.

Losing a beloved pet is heart breaking, because you loved them as family, then you had to let them go. It's so unfair. Just remember how they enriched your life and gave you their unconditional love. You made wonderful memories together, memories that will never leave you.

If I could say one last thing to Ozzy it would be this, "I'm so honored that you chose me as your mummy and you made me so proud every day, sleep tight my little princess. Sleep Tight"

We will always love you ♥

Bud

By

Annetta McDowall

We were considering buying a family pet for some time and wondered which breed of dog to buy, i.e. which would have the right nature for us. My son always wanted a German Shepherd, but we thought maybe that breed would be too big a dog for our little house.

    My husband had been talking to a work mate about it and she had just bought a puppy from breeders who she had two previous dogs from. It just happened to be German Shepherds. She convinced him that their temperament was ideal for us and to go along and see the puppies. We arrived to see the mum and dad who were lovely big dogs and the owner was just lovely. This big fluff ball of a puppy came straight to my son who was sitting on the floor with wide eyes. He climbed up and snuggled into him. Stephen was in love, he had even chosen his name; this is my Bud he told us. We all felt a connection to this wee one. We took him home in the car. He whimpered a little leaving his birth mum but I told him that I would be his mum and love and look after him.

We all had a different relationship with Bud. He came to his mum for affection and love and soothing and also Reiki which he loved.

He went to Stephen, his brother, to play and get up to mischief. He was just another member of the family. I credit Bud with saving my life. I really do. I was diagnosed with depression and anxiety disorder which left me feeling suicidal. I did not want to share how I felt because I was ashamed to be so week. At that time, I thought I should pull myself together. How daft. I did not want to worry my family either with the awful thoughts in my head. With Bud I did not have to say a word. He just appeared to know how I felt and stayed very close to me.

I believe that animal's sense when something is wrong. Bud would just look into my eyes as if he was saying "I'm here, you're going to be OK". No words are needed with dogs and you kind of hide how you feel because they sense it. As I stroked him, anxiety seemed to leave even if it was for a short while. My dog needed to be walked, so I was encouraged to spend time outdoors in the fresh air. This also had a good effect on my mood and Bud smiled at me as we walked. Bud gently encouraged me, kept me going and gave me a purpose to keep going. He similarly helped my son with self- esteem issues He knew that Bud loved him so much that it no longer mattered very much what others thought or said. Having a big wonderful dog seemed to attract new friend and gave him confidence.

I didn't really know that I was losing my big boy but then again I knew something wasn't right. We were flying off on holiday and Bud was going into a kennel. I was doing Reiki for him and found a hot spot. Bud pulled away which was strange because he was a big Reiki dog and loved the energy. I put it to the back of my mind because I just hated to leave him. An over anxious mummy! We were on holiday when Bud died of an aneurism at the kennel.

My son arranged his cremation and an urn for his ashes because I became ill on holiday and was taken to hospital. My son did not want to cause me anymore pain at the time.

On the day he passed I awoke in Turkey to Bud barking. I came home looking for my big Bud wondering where he was hiding. With tears rolling down his face my son told me what had happened. He gave me the urn and hoped that I approved of what he did. My heart broke for my son who had to do this on his own for his beloved dog and brother. My heart broke also because I would never cuddle him again and I wasn't there for his passing. I watched my husband cry out loud as I rocked back and forth in so much pain. I had lost my Mother a few years before and my Father the previous year and I thought I would never feel like that again. I felt this loss equally as painful. I was numb. If you look into the stages of grief my family went through them all. Nowhere in those books or theories do you read about the loss and feeling of grief for a pet.

For weeks it was a struggle to function, there was still the feeling of disbelief, confusion and guilt. Did I know there was something wrong when I did Reiki, when he reacted by pulling away?. He needed his mum and I wasn't there. My poor son had to deal with his loss alone and I wasn't there for him either. I cried when people tried to console me. There were many lovely people who loved Bud too even hid friend the Golden Lab looked for him over and over. It broke my heart when others would comment about him only being a dog.

On a more pleasant note, I have so many wonderful memories of my darling boy. Bud had a great sense of fun and humour. He loved games. We had floor length curtains in our living room and Bud liked to play hide and seek. He would hide behind the curtains all the time wagging his big tail.

We would say "oh where's Bud is he behind the couch?, no, not there, in the kitchen?, no" Bud would pop out with a big smile on his face as if to say "Ta Da!".

If I was to advise anyone after the loss of a beloved pet, it would be to grieve your loss.

You have loved so much and with great love and attachment comes great loss when we part. Don't listen to people who cannot comprehend the pain of losing a pet, it is truly their loss because they have never experienced the love and friendship an animal brings.

To my darling Bud "You are still with us in our hearts and minds. We still love you and that will never end. You have enriched all of our lives; we still look at your pictures and think of you remembering the fun we had. I still feel you with me sometimes my boy, especially when I need strength."

All my love, your mum ♥

Morgan

By

Sarah Wallace

Morgan was from an accidental litter from my sister's cat. My daughter and I had one cat living with us at the time. From the moment we saw the black and white kitten with a black "helmet", we were in love. As the litter grew, I also loved another, a female, who looked just like a snowshoe. Unable to pick just one, we decided the female, who we named 'Hillary' would be mine and Morgan would be my daughter, Mia's kitten. Morgan seemed to have such a great sense of humour for a cat! His sleeping positions for one were a constant source of amusement. He could be stretched out, on his back, on the grass in the middle of the yard, or curled up, high up on the roof of our shed. Morgan absolutely loved dogs, and in particular, our cross-breed rescue dog, Sabrina. He would always be rubbing against her or trying to curl up next to her. Morgan was also a fantastic hunter, much to our dismay at times! He was very proud of what he could do and loved to bring us his handy work, despite our protests!

Morgan wasn't a big people cuddler, though one of his favourite places to sleep was on Mia's bed.

We had only been in our new home just over a month when Morgan went missing.

Even though he was very much an outdoors cat, it wasn't hard to miss his presence; he was always harassing whoever went into the kitchen for his favourite treat, a bowl of milk!

After around four days, I decided to contact a Facebook group of animal communicators, to see if anyone could reach him. A couple of people said he had wandered too far, but was safe, at a house and saw him curled up with another cat, in saying that though, he did say he missed us.

It was when Morgan had been gone for almost 2 weeks when I decided to go for a walk, just calling him and looking. We live in a rural area so our neighbours aren't very close by. I was walking in a neighbouring paddock when I found his poor little body; he was only about two-hundred metres from our home, just off the road, in a ditch. It didn't look like he'd been there long, certainly not two weeks, so I believe he was ok when the communicators talked to him, and that he was probably on his way home. He was so close. My daughter and I were both heartbroken. Morgan's death came at an already sad and stressful period and we just couldn't believe this tragic blow had to come along as well. We had held out hope that he was ok for so long.

Being a dog lover, Morgan loved to go on walks. The majority of his life, we lived on a 180-acre property with our horses. Morgan loved to come on walks to check on or catch the horses, but would get very vocal if he lost sight of us!

A couple of times when riding my horse, I would be about 10 - 15 minutes into my ride, only to realise I had a cat as well as the dogs coming along! I had to make a change in direction and circle back a few times to make sure he didn't get lost, what stamina for a cat!

He would pant like a dog & flop onto the cool grass once we got back, but he was always up to doing it again!

Another distinctive memory of Morgan was his heavy footsteps, I used to joke that he wore boots, because if he came through the house in the night, you could just hear stomp, stomp, stomp, on the floorboards!

Advice to other pet owners going through loss is to try to not feel guilty about whatever has happened, remember the good times and the love you shared, find something nice like a photo or a figurine to have as a memento and keep your heart open for another pet to come into your life when the time is right.

It's hard to know what I'd say to him, I'm sure he knows we still miss him all the time, I'd say "I'm sorry for getting cranky at his hunting antics, because I know he took great pride in it, and I'd say I'm sorry I couldn't keep you safe."

I love you Morgan ♥

Lulu

By

Amy Cheyne

The first time I met my Lulu was when I was working as a receptionist at a vet practice. She had come in as a stray after having been found in a tractor tyre. I knew from the first moment I seen her that we were meant to be together. As rules apply, she had to be taken to the local re-homing centre and kept for a week in kennels in case somebody had lost her.

I went in the week later (after the deadline) and to my amazement she was still there, my heart skipped a beat and I felt like the luckiest person alive to be able to bring my girl home and offer her the loving family life that she so deserved. Our reasoning for getting a second dog was that Sparkie (Lulu's brother) had been feeling lonely so we were looking to get a companion for him (they were the same breed). She filled a very large gap that had been lacking in our lives and before long they were like partners in crime.

One of my fondest memories of Lulu is when she ate my husband's left over kebab that we had bought on the way home from a night out.

We had decided to place the left over's just out the back door to save it stinking up the kitchen. Well, we had forgotten about it by the morning and when we let the dogs out the little tearaway had found it and managed to chew through the polystyrene packaging and eat what was left. Needless to say, we found it funny in a sense and it reminded us of the good deed that we had done in rescuing her from her scavenging days. Lulu was generally healthy in all the years she was with us. It was not until hitting double figures that she became arthritic. We managed it on a daily basis with a drug called Loxicom. She gradually started to deteriorate which led to her being unable to get in and out the back door. This is when we knew that the time had come to say goodbye. We took the heartbreaking decision to have Lulu put to sleep in November 2015. She had been part of our lives since 2003 and had lived to a good age for her breed of nearly fourteen. Not a day goes past that I do not think about my best friend. I miss her dearly and always will. However, I know that deep down we made the right decision as I could no longer see her leading a crippled life as she had been doing just before her time came to an end. There are so many memories that I have of Lulu and cannot choose just one but not seeing her waiting for me at the door now when I come home from work is still very upsetting. My advice to others who have lost a loved pet would be for them to know that their pet will be waiting for them at the other side and until then may they run free over the rainbow bridge until you meet again.

If I could say one thing to my Lulu now it would be "mummy loves and misses you loads and hope that you are being looked after and you are looking after others until the time comes that we are back together."

I love you Lulu ♥

Abbey

By

Jayne Sandford

I first met Abbey at the breeder's house when I went to choose a puppy. I sat on the floor with all ten chocolate Labrador puppies playing with them & observing them to see which puppy I liked the most & which puppy had the type of personality I liked. There was one chocolate Labrador puppy that took a keen interest in myself and walked up to me, sniffed me, got on my knee yawned and went to sleep. As it seemed this puppy was comfortable with me I decided that I would choose her as she had chosen me.

Abbey grew up with my children and she loved to lay next to them when they were playing on the floor, she always alerted me if one of my children became upset and would not rest until I had come to see what the problem was. Abbey would make us laugh when she always knew the best place to sit was under the highchair to catch any food that would drop or thrown to her.

When the sun shone on the carpet in the lounge she would squeeze herself into it just to feel the heat.

She loved the snow so much that by the time I managed to get her to come inside her brown coat was white, just as soon as it snowed she couldn't wait to get outside, she would run around crazy wagging her tail and eating the snow. Abbey loved having her coat brushed and would roll on her back to make sure I didn't forget to rub her belly after having her coat brushed. My children played a game with her where they would crouch on the floor & hide their head and Abbey would try and dig them out until she could get to their face and give them a big lick.

Abbey was seventeen and a half years old and had been unable to walk on her back legs for a while, I bought absorbent disposable bed covers, the type used on children's beds so that she would not be distressed when she went to the toilet as I could remove it quickly, wash and dry her so that she felt okay. I brought her food and water to her and kept to the times she would have had them to keep her life as stress free as I could. Abbey began to refuse her food a few days before I had the most difficult choice I've ever had to make in my life, she would look at me with very sad eyes trying the best she could to tell me that it was her time to go. It took my mum to tell me that I should arrange for the vet to come to the house and put Abbey to sleep as it was her time to go as she did not have a good quality of life anymore and that she seemed very sad. My mum arranged to vet to come & also arranged for Abbey to be picked up after the vet had gone so she could be cremated and her ashes placed in an oak casket.

The day the vet came I didn't know if I was doing the right thing for Abbey right up until they knocked on my door, I cried so much as I was losing a friend who had been my friend for seventeen and half years. Abbey looked at me as they were preparing the injection as if to say 'thank you', I held her head in my arms & cried like a baby as they gave her the injection; and she closed her eyes for the last time, and took her last breath then she was gone forever.

A short while later the pet cremation company came to collect her, she was handled with the utmost dignity as she was transferred onto a small stretcher, put into the back of their van and driven away. Abbey was such a gentle dog that she was more than happy to let our cats get into her basket with her and sleep with her, she would let the cats groom her without batting an eyelid. We loved Abbey so much as she was so much more than our pet she was part of our family and always will be.

One thing I would tell someone that has experienced the loss of their pet is that death is a lie as they never truly leave us as they remain in thoughts and locked within our hearts forever. I would also tell them to expect a visit from their pet as why would they not visit their home, and the people in it who loved them and miss them so much.

If I could speak to Abbey I would ask her if she missed being with us and if she had found my dad who passed to the spirit world before her as he loved her as much as I did and still do. I do speak to Abbey all the time and we do have frequent visits from her, my granddaughter sees her sleeping in the same area that her basket use to be and I have felt her getting herself comfortable at the end of my bed.

I love and miss you Abbey ♥

Elsa

By

Dierdre Golberg

Elsa came into my life as a three week old kitten. An acquaintance contacted me because her female barn cat had been hit by a car and left behind her kittens. She knew I had experience with bottle feeding babies, so she wanted me to take her. Elsa was a joy from the beginning. She was friendly and outgoing even as a little mite. My three year old granddaughter fell in love with her and named her. Elsa was a bit too rambunctious for a house cat (she and her sister Anna tore around the house that first winter and broke many things, including a tall, heavy cactus floor lamp).

So, in the spring Elsa and Anna became the happiest of barn cats. They ran endlessly, climbed trees and hunted for the rodents that love to steal the grain for our horses.

I had been away at a horse rescue clinic one weekend during Elsa's second summer. When I came home, Elsa was not around.

That was not like her at all, she was always there to greet me and follow me around, demanding attention. I felt sick to my stomach and feared the worse. I called, I searched, I pleaded with the universe to tell me what had happened.

    We have coyotes where we live, they might have gotten her. She was so friendly; someone might have seen her by the road and taken her. She might have gotten injured somehow (she was a wild one!) and crawled off to mend. Two weeks passed. I began to smell decomposition in our garage. I had done a pretty through search, but I did another one. I found our dear Elsa behind a panel of wood, gone. Due to her state of decomposition, I did not attempt to look for clues to her demise. I felt so incredibly sad to have lost such a beautiful and vibrant spirit at such a young age. I didn't know I would tell my granddaughter about her beloved cat. I had a tiny bit of relief in at least knowing, but incredible guilt over what I might have done to prevent the loss.

    The funniest memory I have of Elsa, is that shortly after my granddaughter had named she and her sister, I discovered they were boys! It's so hard to sex tiny kittens, and I'd blundered. We did not want to confuse our granddaughter, so we just played along about them being sisters and all the adults got a great kick out of it. I hope they didn't mind.

    The only advice I have for others who have lost their pets is to try to remember the happy times and not dwell on their absence. Find another pet to love and cherish as a tribute to your fallen friend.

    If I could only ask one thing of my Elsa, I would want to know how she died and that I am sorry I wasn't able to help or prevent her leaving.

I will never forget you and I love you♥

Spike

By

Beverley Nuttall

I first saw spike at Pendle bury dogs home, he was a bonny little thing a tad small, with them sad puppy dog eyes, ever so cute. As I looked at him I knew he was the one straight away, I asked to have a hold of him and as they gave him to me, it was love. I said there and then I would have him, filled the paper work out and off we went home. When my son saw him his face lit up, life was good.

Spike changed our life, he was loving, funny & affectionate, one day I took him upstairs to my son and put him on the bed, he had a run around on the bed then decided to jump off the bed, he landed right in the washing basket! Oh we did laugh, he was just funny and a giddy little dog, so playful he just made us smile with happiness. I noticed Spike was putting weight on and then he was weeing more.

So, I took him to the vets, she thought it may have been cushing's, but wasn't sure, so she would have to do some tests, we booked him in for a week later.

He had to stay in all day, after a couple of days we got the phone call from the vet to say yes, it was indeed Cushing's disease. She told me it was a slow progressive illness and that he would have to go on tablets, she said that she wanted to start the tablets on the Monday, but if he was ill, I would need to call an emergency vet out, I explained that we were going away that Monday for nearly a month and my husband's daughter was looking after Spike & Scruff. She advised me to wait until I came back to start the tablets, which we did when we came back. I noticed that Spike had lost weight and booked him in to the vets for the Tuesday (as we had got back on the Monday)

    I got up on the Tuesday morning, let the dogs out, but noticed spike was drinking dirty water. I shouted them in, but then spike wouldn't drink the fresh water which was strange. I went to work at 7.45am, got an appointment with the vets at 9.30am so went home to collect Spike, as I walked in expecting Spike to greet me as he always did, but he never greeted me at the door. I went in the front room and he was lying on the floor, he had pooed on the floor and he was breathing ever so slow, I picked him up and rushed to the vet. I rang my son and told him to get to the vets as soon as possible, the vet said it was probably a blood clot that had moved, so she said she could put Spike on a drip, but didn't think it would help, my son made the decision to let spike go peacefully.

    At the time you do wonder why my dog? What if I did this and what if I did that, but then you remind yourself it was a blood clot and there would have been nothing you could have done.

    After Spike had gone, my house felt so empty, even though I still have scruff, scruff didn't eat for days, he was so very sad, he would keep looking at the front door, when I took him out, he kept turning round looking for spike, eight months down the line the house still feels empty, I miss Spike every day, I talk to him every day.

Memories I have of Spike are jumping off the bed into the washing basket, we did laugh.
And chewing all my wall paper off as a pup, there are so many lovely memories.

If I could give any advice to others, is talk to any one that will listen about your pet, it does help, well it helps me. If I could say something to him now it would be; "I love you, I miss you and everyone else misses you too, we would give anything to have one more day with you."

I love you Spike ♥

Moose

By

Lilliana Roselaie

I wasn't really looking at getting a second dog, but thought that the dog we had might like a mate as he was a bit aloof despite our doting, so I browsed a pet re-homing page to see if the idea felt like a good solution. Browsing the pictures of needy dogs it occurred the idea would only add problems, however a second later the picture of Moose came into view and I was instantly drawn to him. It didn't matter what words were written on his bio, I wanted to make him mine. Given up due to a medical condition, he was a needy dog, but I found myself overlooking every possible adversity and making room in my life and heart for him.

Insistently, I convinced the Dalmatian rescue organisation I would provide the best possible home and I was granted permission to adopt him despite the 2,200km distance he would need to travel.

Upon collecting him from the airport our bond was instant, he was mine and I was his.

While Moose did get on well with our other Dalmatian, it was clear it was only my company he craved for. Moose was always by my side, no matter what I was doing or where I was going. His desire to be near me and my desire to have him with me saw us do everything together. We went everywhere together and were very seldom apart, my whole life accommodated him in every way. He was my partner and every night he would share my bed, often we would fall asleep snuggling or holding his paw in my hand. Moose craved so much love and affection, there was never a limit to how much love he wanted to receive and give back in return. Never in my whole life had I ever felt so loved by anyone and I loved him more than life itself.

Moose meant so much to me I was extremely protective of him, I could not bear the thought of any possibility that could take him from me. However, I knew I was powerless to prevent old age, but that did not stop me from trying; it was half way into his lifespan when I hoped for some crazy scientific way to give us more time. Knowing it was science fiction I began to make every moment with him count as even though it was years away yet. I knew our time was finite. One day while on a walk his back legs buckled, my eyes welled knowing this was the first sign of age at twelve years. I did everything I could to slow it down, changed our routine and made life easier for him and he was ok for another three and half years. Suddenly he deteriorated with his back legs buckling once again, again I tried everything holding hope with a surgical procedure, but nothing could stop the degeneration in his spine.

The day came when he could no longer support his body even with assistance to toilet. I had to make the hardest decision of my entire life; I made the appointment with the vet for the following day.

My family supported me and gave Moose a special last day, filled with all his favourite food and things; I had a home service come to our house. As the afternoon sun was fading, I lay down on the bed with him holding him in my arms. It took every ounce of my strength to calmly whisper in his ear that it was ok for him to go now because inside I was falling apart my heart breaking and dying. He took his last three breaths and the sound and sight is forever burned into mind. The vet took him away as I had arranged a cremation service for him. For the first few days I was totally lost, however it was a big comfort when he was returned home to me. In the weeks that followed I felt a combination of numbness and denial, I could not accept he was gone, I could not clean up any of his things, I wanted his hair still on the carpet, his bucket of water in the corner. Every night I cried endless tears and my sleep was filled with nightmares, I found the worst part for me was the guilt of having to end his life even though I know it was to prevent him suffering, the guilt was overwhelming. The absence of him was an all-consuming void like nothing I have ever felt before and really has no words able to describe it. At times his loss has been incapacitating as life without him is hard to accept, he was such a significant part. I have found comfort in acknowledging that significance, I keep his bowl in the same place, a bag of his food still in the cupboard, his coat still on the hanger and his lead still on the hook.

For weeks after I could feel his presence still with me, until one night he came to me in a dream, told me to stop being so sad, in the dream he showed me another dog, when I looked into the eyes of the dog it was his eyes. I feel he was showing me that we will be together again sometime in the future.

I will love you forever Moose ♥

THE END

Joannes final words

Well, we are at the end of this book and I do hope you have enjoyed and probably cried a little at the stories so lovingly expressed in this book. Everyone who contributed here wanted so deeply to not only help you, but to keep their animals memories alive. Their legacy will live on forever.

If you are suffering loss yourself, know that we understand just how difficult it is and would love nothing more than to offer you a little support. Firstly, feel free to come and find us on Facebook where we can help you during those difficult times. Also, know that there are some very clear stages of grief that you will naturally go through, I will list them for you in order that you can spot the signs, and allow yourself to heal. No one said it would ever be easy, but just remember that you had the absolute pleasure of a deep heartfelt bond with your animal that some people never experience in their lifetime. You were truly blessed.

I wish you swift recovery from your Grief and hope you find that bond again very soon. Light and happiness will shine upon you once again.

Love and light

Joanne Hull

WWW.JOANNEHULL.COM

Stages of Grief and How to Overcome them

We all have our own ways of dealing with grief, a person who heals quickly may not have loved their dog any less than that of someone who takes months, if not years to come to terms with the loss. No two people are the same and it's down to the individual to decide when they are at peace with their loss.

Never allow anyone to say it was 'Just a dog' or 'Just a cat' these beautiful creatures were living, breathing sentient beings, who could love, grieve, feel pain, anger and share a heart bond like nothing else, we call this 'un-conditional love'. Something so very special, that it compares to nothing ever experienced.

So, you are not alone, here I have listed the stages of grief, follow how you feel and refer to the explanations, it can help you understand the natural process the body must go through in order to heal.

Some people will seem okay one minute, then slip back through the stages over and over, there is no set rule, it takes as long as it takes, be kind to yourself.

DENIAL
GUILT
ANGER
DEPRESSION
CLOSURE

DENIAL
Denial is a form of protection, a defense mechanism that our brains can use in an attempt to protect ourselves from the emotional trauma of losing a loved one.

We may convince ourselves that what is happening or about to happen simply can't be true. Or that what we may be hearing from our vet is wrong. Put simply, denial is a refusal to accept the truth.

GUILT
Is the most common feeling of all, in my opinion having to make that dreadful decision to end your animal's life, is just terrible. Even if it truly is the best option, it will be one of the worst decisions you are ever likely to make.

Feelings of guilt can overwhelm us so much that we are unable to function. We may find ourselves asking 'Did I do the right thing?' 'Was it the right time?' 'What if I made a mistake?' 'Did I make him suffer?' etc and this guilt will continue to traumatize you until you move into the next grief stage.

ANGER
Is one of the most common stages of grief, it may be aimed at the vet who you feel may not have saved your dog or helped you as much as you feel you should have been. At friends, who offer advice, or at family members, who are just trying to help. Sometimes anger can be directed at ourselves as a form of guilt and in some cases even directed at the animal itself for leaving you.

DEPRESSION
Is not unusual when grieving our lost animals, for many of us including myself, losing a pet is one of the saddest experiences we ever have to experience and depression can develop at any time and to varying degrees.

We may feel a lack of interest in the outside world and find it difficult to concentrate, eat, sleep and carry out even the most normal of daily tasks.

The help and understanding of other people is absolutely essential at this time and yet we may want to remove ourselves from them. It has been medically proven that talking through your grief with someone else not only help the healing process begin, but also enables you to move forward and accept what has happened.

CLOSURE
Is the final and most significant stage of the pet grieving process. At this point owners are able to accept that their beloved pet has died. We can finally begin to focus on the happy times we once shared together. Remembering how funny, cute and full of love our pets were. The owner may even consider looking for a new animal. This will never replace the pet that has passed but it may fill an emotional space within us that the old pet has left behind.

The anger, sadness or guilt may still occur, but are likely to pass more quickly than before. This is the time to look forward and renew that sense of un-conditional love that our animals give us. We all need to create a way to find closure whether by planting a tree in memory of our loved pet or perhaps having a painting done of the animal. Some people like to scatter their animal's ashes in a place they both shared good times together. Out on a favourite walk or on the beach or in the woods perhaps.

Finding a way to remember the good times you shared together is paramount. However you choose to commemorate them, peace and remembrance will be sure to follow. And life without your animal will become much easier to accept. Without closure we are unable to fully draw a line under our stages of grief.

Acknowledgements

This book could not have been written without all my wonderful Facebook followers from around the world who so bravely told their stories and to those precious animals that we have lost to the world of spirit. The animals who touched our hearts beyond measure. And to Claire Allen, who so gracefully stepped up as my proof reader, I will be forever grateful ☺ Thanks Claire! x

A special thank you to Dave my partner who so lovingly supported the making of this book and made sure I was topped up with coffee throughout! Thanks Dave x

I pray we sell more of this book than we could ever imagine and in doing so we raise much needed funds to help so many more animals, by sharing the details of this books availability, you are joining a worldwide family of animal lovers who just wish to do something super special for the animal kingdom. And for that we all thank you.

To all the animals that are out there in the world, this book is a tribute for your beauty, intelligence and sheer love you offer so freely.

Your hearts will live on forever! ♥

Joanne Hull

Details of Joanne's workshops, worldwide speaking engagements, TV appearances and learning opportunities, so you too can learn the art of Animal Communication, including Joanne's Home Learning Course which can all be found on Joanne's website **www.joannehull.com**

MORE BOOKS BY JOANNE HULL

THE PET PSYCHIC
JOANNE HULL

They speak, she listens

Her amazing life story and tales from the world of animal communication

Joanne Hull always knew that there was something that made her different from other children

While other girls her age were playing with dolls, Joanne was busy collecting any stray animal that came her way, until her parent's back yard resembled a zoo. As she grew older she realized that she was developing incredible powers that allowed her to physically connect with and talk to animals

For many years Joanne has used the animal spirit world to help owners across the world understand troubled pets, finding missing ones and most amazingly contact those we have lost to the other side. Joanne has given hundreds of spine chilling accurate readings and for the first time she shares the sometimes heart warming and sometimes heartbreaking but always extraordinary stories that have formed her life as THE PET PSYCHIC.

Available from all good Bookstores & Online.

PUPPY TALES
JOANNE HULL

Heart warming true stories of man's best friend

Ever since she was a child, Joanne Hull has had an unusual affinity with animals and an incredible ability to communicate with them. Unsurprisingly, this connection is particularly strong with man's best friend. Intelligent, loving and loyal, dogs have always had a unique bond with humans and a special place in many people's hearts.

For years Joanne Hull has been a dedicated dog owner and has helped other owners across the world understand their pets. In this book Joanne shares funny, heart warming and sometimes heartbreaking stories, and offers practical advice on how people can improve communication with their own canine companion.

From uplifting tales of heroic dogs who saved the day to hilarious dog related dilemmas and moving accounts of precious pets who are no longer with us. Puppy Tales is a celebration of all our four pawed friends and a revelation in how to really understand your dog.

Available from all good Bookshops & Online

BOOKS BY JOANNE

The Pet Psychic

Puppy Tales

A Whisper away

Animal Communication -*The complete guide*

Paws from the Past

www.joannehull.com

Printed in Great Britain
by Amazon